Providing Child Care to Military Families

The Role of the Demand Formula in Defining Need and Informing Policy

Joy S. Moini, Gail L. Zellman, Susan M. Gates

Prepared for the Office of the Secretary of Defense

RAND NATIONAL DEFENSE RESEARCH INSTITUTE

The research described in this report was prepared for the Office of the Secretary of Defense (OSD). The research was conducted in the RAND National Defense Research Institute, a federally funded research and development center sponsored by the OSD, the Joint Staff, the Unified Combatant Commands, the Department of the Navy, the Marine Corps, the defense agencies, and the defense Intelligence Community under Contract DASW01-01-C-0004.

Library of Congress Cataloging-in-Publication Data

Providing child care to military families : the role of the demand formula in defining need and informing policy / Joy S. Moini, Gail L. Zellman, Susan M. Gates.
p. cm.
"MG-387."
Includes bibliographical references.
ISBN 0-8330-3927-X (pbk. : alk. paper)
1. Children of military personnel—Care—United States. 2. United States. Dept. of Defense—Officials and employees—Salaries, etc. 3. Employer-supported day care—United States. 4. Day care centers—United States. I. Moini, Joy S. II. Zelman, Gail. III. Gates, Susan M., 1968– .

UB403.P768 2006
362.71'202435500973—dc22

2006018408

Published 2006 by the RAND Corporation
1776 Main Street, P.O. Box 2138, Santa Monica, CA 90407-2138
1200 South Hayes Street, Arlington, VA 22202-5050
4570 Fifth Avenue, Suite 600, Pittsburgh, PA 15213-2665
RAND URL: http://www.rand.org/
To order RAND documents or to obtain additional information, contact
Distribution Services: Telephone: (310) 451-7002;
Fax: (310) 451-6915; Email: order@rand.org

Preface

The Office of the Secretary of Defense asked the RAND Corporation to assess the Department of Defense (DoD) child-care demand formula and recommend improvements to it. RAND's recommendations, which are presented in this document, are based on the results of a survey of military families conducted in 2004 and focus groups convened with military parents in 2003.

This monograph is intended to provide DoD policymakers and managers of the military child-care system with information on the validity of the DoD formula, to improve the understanding of the factors that influence key child-care outcomes, and to address the broader issue of how DoD might refine its goals for military child care.

This monograph is the sixth in a series of RAND reports on military child care. The first, *Improving the Delivery of Military Child Care: An Analysis of Current Operations and New Approaches* (R-4145-FMP, 1992), examined military child-care operations prior to the implementation of the Military Child Care Act (MCCA) of 1989. The second, *Examining the Effects of Accreditation on Military Child Development Center Operations and Outcomes* (MR-524-OSD, 1994), analyzed a key aspect of the MCCA: accreditation of child-care centers. The third, *Examining the Implementation and Outcomes of the Military Child Care Act of 1989* (MR-665-OSD, 1998), analyzed the many changes that the MCCA brought about. The fourth, *Examining the Cost of Military Child Care* (MR-1415-OSD, 2002), determined the cost of providing care in military child-development centers and family child-care homes. A fifth report, *Examining Child Care Need Among Military Families* (TR-279-OSD, 2006), is a companion technical report to this monograph. It provides an analysis of unmet need for care, unmet preference for care, and several other child-care outcomes. For those who are interested in the analytic techniques used in this study, the technical report provides a description of the study's focus groups, survey methodology, and survey results.

This research was sponsored by the Department of Defense Office of Children and Youth and was conducted within the Forces and Resources Policy Center of the RAND National Defense Research Institute (NDRI). NDRI, a division of the RAND Corporation, is a federally funded research and development center sponsored by the Office of the Secretary of Defense, the Joint Staff, the Unified Combatant Commands, the Department of the Navy, the Marine Corps, the defense agencies, and the defense Intelligence Community.

Comments and questions on this document may be directed to the authors—Joy Moini at moini@rand.org and Gail Zellman and Susan Gates at the RAND Corporation, 1776 Main Street, Santa Monica, CA 90407-2138. For more information on RAND's Forces and Resources Policy Center, contact the Director, James Hosek. He can be reached by email at James_Hosek@rand.org; by phone at 310-393-0411, extension 7183; or by mail at the RAND Corporation, 1776 Main Street, Santa Monica, CA 90407-2138. More information about RAND is available at http://www.rand.org.

Contents

APPENDIX

Figures

Tables

Summary

The Department of Defense (DoD) is committed to meeting the need for child care among military families. DoD supports the largest employer-sponsored system of high-quality child care in the country. Through accredited child development centers (CDCs), family child care (FCC) homes,[1] youth centers, and other after-school programs, DoD currently provides approximately 176,000 child-care spaces for military children 0–12 years old and plans to expand this capacity to 215,412 spaces by fiscal year 2007.[2]

DoD recognizes that high-quality child care is both a readiness issue and a retention issue. Difficulty in obtaining child care creates conflicts between parental obligations and mission responsibilities, and if parents have no child care, they may fail to report for duty in order to care for their children. If parents are forced to make informal child-care arrangements, they may perceive that care to be of low quality and may be distracted from their work as a result. For families with an employed civilian spouse, inadequate child care may affect the spouse's career options and ultimately the family's decision to stay in the military.

To estimate the magnitude of child-care need among military service personnel, DoD uses a formula incorporating installation-level and other demographic data, including a combination of national

---

1 FCC is child care provided in a person's home. A CDC is a dedicated facility. All U.S. states license child-care providers (both CDCs and FCCs). A DoD FCC is an FCC that has been approved by DoD.

2 There are approximately 1.2 million children of military parents, according to DoD estimates. See the Military HOMEFRONT Web site (http://www.mfrc-dodqol.org/MCY/mm_cdc.htm, last accessed August 11, 2005).

and military statistical trends. Because the formula is based solely on demographic data, DoD was concerned that the formula might not be addressing all relevant aspects of child-care need.

The Office of the Secretary of Defense asked the RAND Corporation to assess the validity of the DoD formula as a tool for translating information on military families into measures of potential child-care need and to suggest ways that the tool might be improved. RAND was also asked to clarify the role of the formula in DoD child-care policy decisions and to improve understanding of the factors that influence key child-care outcomes of interest to aid DoD in refining its goals for military child care. To perform this assessment, researchers conducted focus groups on eight installations and developed a survey to assess parental preferences and other factors that might affect child-care need. The survey was sent to a sample of 3,000 families of active-duty military members, including activated reservists, stationed in the United States who reported having dependent children age 12 or younger as of September 2003. The survey asked military parents about their child-care arrangements, unmet needs for care, unmet preferences for care, and the effect of child-care issues on their readiness and intention to remain in the military.

Some Aspects of the DoD Child-Care Demand Formula Deserve Attention

The RAND analyses indicate that some aspects of the formula deserve attention and revision. The DoD child-care "demand formula" is actually a formula for determining *potential need* for child care among military families. The formula relies on data from the Defense Manpower Data Center (DMDC), Defense Enrollment Eligibility Reporting System (DEERS), and from the services, and assumptions about the fraction of dependent children living with their parents in different family types (single parent, dual military, military member with civilian spouse) to estimate potential need. The estimate derived from the formula represents an upper bound on the number of DoD-sponsored child-care spaces required to meet the needs of military families. This number is then considered in light of available resources and competing demands to arrive at a goal for the amount of child-care spaces the system should provide. Because some families will choose to use non-DoD care (including parental and family care), the actual need for child care will be less than the potential need calculated by the formula.

The results of the RAND survey suggest that there may be problems with the accuracy of inputs to the formula, particularly some of the DEERS data inputs. Because the child-care formula makes fundamentally different assumptions about the potential need for child care among families of different types, accurate estimates of the family status of military members with minor dependents are critical to determining child-care need, but, as we found, they are often flawed. This study found substantial differences between family status reported in DEERS and family status reported by survey respondents. Of those families identified by DEERS as a "single-parent family," only 51 percent reported single-parent status. Similarly, only 83 percent of those identified by DEERS as "military married to civilian" families and 90 percent identified as "dual-military" families reported having the same status as in the DEERS data. In addition, because DEERS no longer includes a flag denoting dual-military families, identifying this family type proved to be quite challenging.

The survey results also raise questions about some of the formula's assumptions regarding use of child care among different family types. Specifically, the assumptions made by the formula about the fraction of children living with military parents and about spousal employment rates differed substantially from what was found from the survey.

Multiple Child-Care Indicators Provide Important Insights into How Well the System Is Working

There are other important child-care indicators besides potential need that the DoD should consider as "intermediate" child-care system outcomes. They include child-care use and the need for multiple sources of care, unmet need for care, and unmet preference for care (i.e., a family is not using its preferred type of care). Ultimately, the DoD child-care system must be assessed in terms of the support it provides to desired outcomes for the military. Readiness, particularly time lost to duty because of child-care problems, and the degree to which child care plays a role in a military member's propensity to leave the service represent two crucial "final" system outcomes that our survey results highlight.

DoD CDC users appear to have a weaker attachment to the military. Our survey reveals that CDC users are more likely than users of other types of care to report a high probability of leaving the military due to child-care issues. This finding is surprising, given that DoD CDC care is the most sought-after as well as the most heavily subsidized type of non-parental child care. One must be careful not to interpret this finding as causal, i.e., that it suggests that CDC care *causes* families to contemplate leaving the military. It may be that the families who use a CDC are families who find it more challenging to balance family obligations and military duty. Nonetheless, the greater propensity to leave the military due to child-care issues that was reported by DoD CDC users suggests that DoD may want to take steps to better understand the attitudes and needs of CDC families.

Families that are living off base are less likely to use DoD-sponsored care. The distance between a family's home and an installation is strongly related to the type of child care the family uses. Families living off base are less likely to use DoD-sponsored child-care options, and the propensity to use DoD-sponsored care decreases the farther a family lives from the base. This suggests that the housing patterns of military families stationed on a particular installation are important factors for the DoD to consider in deciding how to allocate its child-care resources.

Local market conditions are related to the child-care choices that DoD families make. This analysis revealed that families with preschool-age children who live in areas with lower median incomes are more likely to use civilian child care. DoD may want to consider characteristics of the local community in determining the relative need for DoD-sponsored care so that child-care resources can be most effectively allocated.

Unmet child-care need is not prevalent among military families. Just under 10 percent of military families report unmet child-care need. Unmet need is much more prevalent among families with preschool-age than school-age children, those with a civilian working spouse, and those earning less than $50,000 per year. These findings indicate that two of the biggest gaps in care continue to be in providing care to preschool-age children and ensuring the affordability of care for lower-income families.

Unmet preference is more common than unmet need. Twenty-two percent of military families report unmet preference for child care, with a greater prevalence of unmet preference among families with pre-school-age children. Overall, 54 percent of the families who reported unmet preference stated that they would prefer some form of care provided by DoD, while 46 percent of families would prefer something other than what DoD currently provides. The latter finding suggests that DoD may want to consider developing additional ways of supporting child care to better meet the child-care preferences of military families.

Child-care issues impact the readiness of military members. The survey found that child-care issues impact the readiness of military members to varying degrees. Single-parent and dual-military families with preschool-age children reported challenges in finding child care after the birth of the child that was specifically inquired about in the survey or after moving to an installation that prevented those families from reporting for military duty. Single parents in particular report long search times for child-care arrangements. The impact of child-care issues appears to be greater for female than for male military members. While deployments have some effect on child-care arrangements for all DoD families, finding care after returning from deployment was not reported to be a significant problem among most DoD families; single-parent families are the exception. These families may need additional support post-deployment.

Child-care concerns may influence retention decisions. Previous research (cited in Chapter Four) suggests a possible link between child-care issues and retention. Our survey provides more-direct evidence of a relationship between child-care problems and retention decisions. More than one-fifth of survey respondents reported that it is likely or very likely that child-care issues would lead them to leave the military. Families with preschool-age children are much more likely to report such a propensity than are families with school-age children. Among family types, dual-military and single-parent families are much more likely than those with a non-working civilian spouse to report such a propensity, when controlling for family type, than are families using CDC care.

Policy Options for DoD to Consider

Our research reveals that child care is a potentially important retention and readiness issue, not only for military members who are married to civilian spouses but also for single military parents and dual-military families.

DoD should focus on other child-care outcomes in addition to potential need. Currently, DoD relies on its child-care demand formula as the basis for policymaking related to child-care issues, and particularly for establishing the number of spaces the DoD child-care system should provide. But this formula calculates only potential need. Potential need must be considered along with other, intermediate outcomes, such as actual child-care need and child-care use; all of these measures are ways to understand the effects of child care on key child-care system outcomes, military readiness, and the propensity to leave the military.

To deploy resources in the most effective manner, DoD must clarify its goals for the military child-care system and identify the key outcomes of interest. Then, with these objectives in mind, DoD can meaningfully translate potential need to the number of spaces in selected care settings that it should provide. Figure S.1 illustrates the general relationships that frame the relationship between potential need, intermediate outcomes, and final outcomes for child care, and policy responses that DoD can use to meet its goals.

Figure S.1
Child-Care Outcomes and Potential Policy Responses

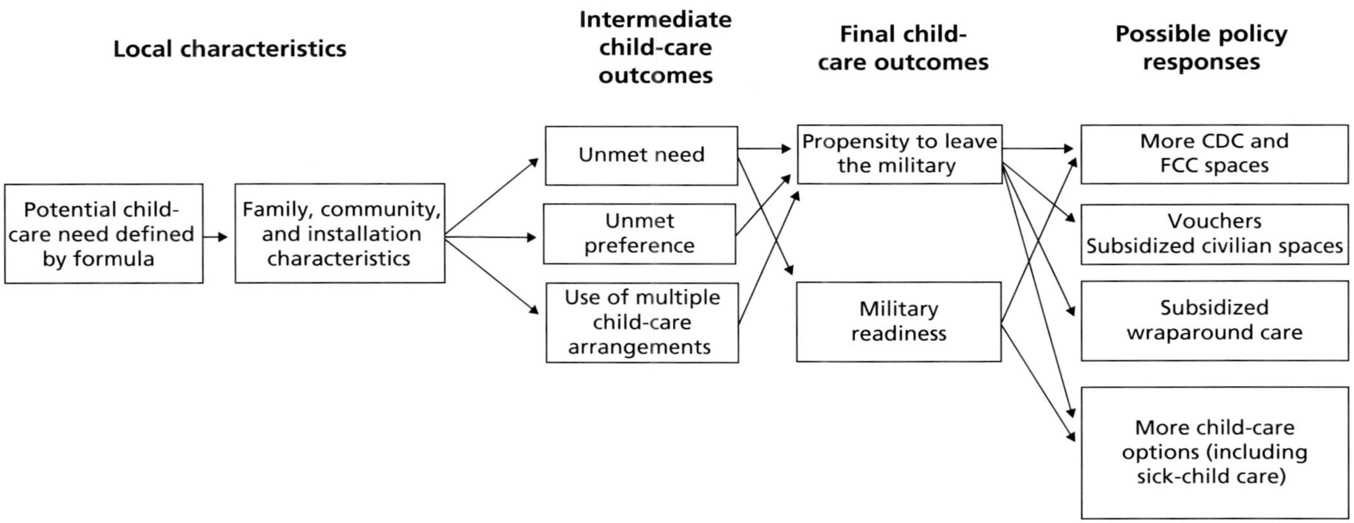

RAND *MG387-S.1*

DoD should clarify which child-care outcomes are of greatest concern, and those outcomes should drive the system. It is critical that DoD identify goals for the military child-care system and establish the key outcomes of interest. For example, one goal might be to reduce the level of unmet preference as much as possible. Another might be to reduce the level of unmet need or to reduce the number of workdays lost by military personnel due to child-care problems.

DoD should give consideration to installation-specific characteristics that influence child-care outcomes and effective policy responses. DoD's current formula does not take into account key installation characteristics that the study data indicate impact multiple child-care outcomes. Because families who live on or near an installation are more inclined to use and to prefer on-base DoD-sponsored CDCs and FCC, an installation with limited on- and near-base housing is likely to face lower actual need for on-base child care. To address unmet need on such an installation, DoD might consider subsidizing care in civilian-operated centers or providing vouchers in those communities where military families actually live. Analogously, in communities with a low cost of living, families prefer civilian care because it is cheaper for most of them. To address unmet need in these communities, DoD may want to reduce the number of DoD-sponsored spaces and use those resources to subsidize wraparound care that will fill in the child-care gaps for families whose duty hours extend beyond the operating hours of civilian centers so that parents can avoid missing duty.

DoD should consider creating more policy alternatives in the child-care arena. A major difficulty in selecting outcomes of choice is that, currently, DoD has few policy levers in the child-care arena. The key policy lever is the number of spaces available for care in DoD-sponsored child-care settings. Additional policy alternatives, along with greater flexibility in applying them at the installation level, could improve child-care outcomes. Depending on the local circumstances, policy alternatives might include child-care vouchers, subsidized spaces in civilian centers, subsidized wraparound care, or support for after-school programs in the community. DoD recently introduced a new program called "Operation: Military Child Care" that can serve as an example of the type of policy option DoD might want to pursue further. The program seeks to aid active-duty, reserve, and National Guard families who do not have access to DoD-sponsored care on base to locate child care, and it will defray the cost of that care while military members of the families are mobilized or deployed. Clear DoD guidance, combined with a package of policy options that extends beyond creating spaces in DoD-sponsored care, holds the promise of better utilization of child-care resources to promote DoD's goals and provide families with more care choices and greater well-being for their children.

DoD should collect additional data to improve the formula's predictions and better target child-care resources. As stated earlier, our survey data do not closely match DEERS designations of family type. Certainly, marriage and divorce are dynamic, and our survey response rate was low. But family type is a key child-care demand formula variable; we urge DoD to conduct DEERS validation studies to ensure that the data that populate the formula are producing the most accurate indicators possible. For similar reasons, DoD should reinstate the dual-military flag in the DEERS data. In addition, collection of data on installation housing patterns and local markets would help to better target child-care resources.

A DoD-wide role may be needed to allocate child-care resources effectively. Our survey results suggest that there is no one-size-fits-all approach that can effectively address the child-care needs of DoD families. The survey results also suggest that potential need, as characterized by the DoD formula, can best be met with a range of child-care options. While the formula provides a useful starting point for predicting child-care need, installation characteristics, in particular the average income of the local community and the housing decisions of military families, appear to have important implications for the type of care used and the need for DoD-operated child-care spaces as opposed to other options, such as subsidized care in the community.

Currently, there is no mechanism for the centralized determination of child-care needs across installations. Individual commanders, or in some cases the services, decide how to allocate funding for the construction and operation of CDCs. This leads to tremendous variation in the level of child-care availability across installations. Higher-level consideration of child-care needs across installations, combined with the use of a broader set of policy tools, could lead to more options that would promote the military's ultimate goals: readiness and retention.

Acknowledgments

We would like to thank all of the military families who took the time to fill out the military child-care survey and participate in our focus groups. This research would not have been possible without their input.

We are indebted to our sponsors, Jan Witte and Barbara Thompson of the Office of Children and Youth in the Department of Defense. We appreciate their support in all aspects of the project and their valuable feedback and guidance following interim presentations of our work.

Scott Seggerman and Kit Tong of DMDC provided us with access to data on military families with dependent children and drew the survey sample for us. Our complicated sample design required a lot of hard work on their part, and we are indebted to them for that effort.

We would like to thank RAND colleagues Jennifer Hawes-Dawson, who effectively managed the fielding of the survey; Jon Scott, who cleaned the data and set up the data files; and Jennifer Kavanagh, who re-coded some of the variables after the survey was completed. Ashlesha Datar and Laura Castaneda provided helpful reviews of a draft version of this report.

Donna White and Christopher Dirks provided secretarial support. Kristin Leuschner helped to revise sections of an earlier version of this document to improve its readability.

Acronyms

CDC	child development center
DEERS	Defense Enrollment Eligibility Reporting System
DMDC	Defense Manpower Data Center
DoD	Department of Defense
FCC	family child care
MCCA	Military Child Care Act of 1989
MILCON	military construction
NAEYC	National Association for the Education of Young Children
OSD	Office of the Secretary of Defense
RAPIDS	Real-Time Automated Personnel Identification Card System
SAC	school-age care (DoD)

CHAPTER ONE

Introduction

The Department of Defense (DoD) supports the largest employer-sponsored system of high-quality child care in the country. Through accredited child development centers (CDCs), family child care (FCC) homes,[1] youth centers, and other after-school programs, the DoD provides approximately 176,000 spaces for military children age 0–12, according to the DoD Office of Family Policy.[2] Yet, despite the vast size of the system, access to military child care is far from universal within the DoD. Many families remain on waiting lists for military child care or seek alternatives off base. The DoD recognizes that high-quality child care is both a readiness issue and a retention issue. Lack of child care creates conflicts between parental and mission responsibilities; if parents have no child care, they may be absent from duty in order to care for their children. If parents are forced to make informal child-care arrangements, they may be worried that this care is of low quality and be distracted from duty as a result. If parents must address such problems frequently, it may make remaining in the military unfeasible.

---

[1] FCC is child care provided in a person's home. A CDC is a dedicated facility. All U.S. states license child-care providers (both CDCs and FCCs). A DoD FCC is an FCC that has been approved by DoD. Most installations will only approve military spouses operating an FCC in an on-base home. But, increasingly, installations are moving to approve off-base FCCs as well (usually those run by military spouses or the spouses of retired military).

[2] See the Military HOMEFRONT Web site, http://www.mfrc-dodqol.org/MCY/mm_cdc.htm (last accessed March 23, 2005).

High-quality care allows parents to focus their attention on their work; available care at reasonable cost enables spouses to work, thus increasing family income and allowing spouses to pursue careers. Still, DoD policymakers remain concerned that the system falls short of meeting the needs of military families with children.[3] Over the years, the DoD has tried to quantify the need for child care among military families and to use that information to establish specific targets for the number of DoD-sponsored child-care spaces needed. These child-care need targets have varied over the years, both in terms of numbers and the way in which these targets are determined. Early on, targets were described as percentages (e.g., the system should aim to meet 75 percent of the child-care need); in recent years, targets have been expressed in numbers of spaces. The current goal is to provide 215,412 spaces by fiscal year 2007. Regardless of how the goal is stated, the DoD is interested in ensuring that military families have access to high-quality, affordable child care. To evaluate how well the current system meets that objective, the DoD needs information on the magnitude of the potential need for care.

To estimate the magnitude of child-care need among military service personnel, the DoD uses a formula incorporating installation-level and other demographic data, including "a combination of national and military statistical trends to determine the number of potential child care users" (Jehn, 1990). These data include the number of dependent children who are part of single-parent families, dual-military families, or families with a military member and a civilian spouse; the number

---

[3] One reason for such concern is the persistence of waiting lists for DoD-sponsored care on military bases. However, it is widely recognized that waiting lists are an imperfect measure of the need for child care. In 1992, the DoD required installations to maintain several different waiting lists for DoD-provided care. There is a list for families with *unmet need,* defined for the purposes of the waiting list as those families in which a parent cannot work because of lack of care, or those families that are using unsatisfactory care that is costly (determined as 20 percent more than the highest DoD fee category) or that is unlicensed. There is another list for families with *unmet preference,* defined as those families with a satisfactory child-care arrangement but who wish to have another kind of care. Parents may be reluctant to place their children on certain waiting lists because they are too long. Conversely, people may remain on a list even after they have found an alternative care arrangement.

of families with civilian spouses working outside the home full time and part time or attending school; and the number of DoD civilians working on the installation.

Because the formula is based solely on demographic data, the DoD was concerned that the formula might not be addressing all relevant aspects of child-care need. The Office of the Secretary of Defense (OSD) asked the RAND Corporation to assess the validity of its demand formula and to recommend improvements. As an initial step in this process, RAND conducted 21 focus groups at eight installations. On the basis of those focus groups, RAND developed a military child-care survey designed to better understand parental preferences and other factors that may affect child-care need.

This report uses the results of the focus groups and the analysis of the survey data to evaluate the DoD's child-care demand formula both as a mechanism for translating basic demographic characteristics of military members into some measure of potential child-care need and as a policy tool for assisting the DoD in meeting the child-care needs of military families. This report provides DoD policymakers and managers of the military child-care system with information on the validity of the DoD formula, analyzes the factors that influence key child-care outcomes, and addresses the broader issue of how the DoD can refine its goals for military child care. A related RAND technical report (Gates et al., 2006) provides a detailed overview of the military child-care survey and an analysis of the survey results. In the remainder of this chapter, we provide an overview of the military child-care system and describe in more detail the current formula the DoD uses to assess child-care need. We also describe our approach to conducting our analyses.

The Military Child-Care System

Military child care is provided as part of a system of care designed to meet the needs of military families as children age, so that children can be served by the DoD child-care system from age six weeks until age 12. A range of different settings enables the system to meet parents' needs for reliable, high-quality care while recognizing parental preferences concerning environment, size, and flexibility. The military provides care for as much as 12 hours a day in CDCs, and even longer if necessary in FCC homes.[4] For those families with more-limited need, care may also be provided on a part-time and an hourly basis in CDCs and FCC homes in many locations. Before- and after-school programs are available to care for school-age children in a center-like setting; youth programs provide a relatively unstructured but supervised setting.

The System Provides Significant Subsidies for CDC Use

Within the military child-care system, different types of care are subsidized at dramatically different rates (see Zellman and Gates, 2002). The term *subsidy* has different meanings for different types of care. For CDC care, it reflects the difference between the cost to DoD of providing the care and the price charged to parents. It is important to note that, for military child care, the subsidy is usually not visible to parents; while weekly CDC fees are well below market rates in every fee category, parents may not be aware of the substantially higher fees for comparable care in the civilian sector. For FCC care, the subsidy reflects a payment from the DoD to FCC providers, which often covers only insurance or other incidentals, or is designed to promote a DoD goal, such as increased infant care. This payment supplements parent fees, but is not typically visible to parents because it is provided directly to the provider. For civilian care, a subsidy would reflect a payment from the DoD to the civilian provider to supplement parent fees. This type of subsidy would be more visible to parents, and particularly so if the subsidy were delivered in the form of a voucher.

In the DoD system, CDC care is highly subsidized, while there are only limited subsidies for FCC care and, in most cases, no subsidy for non-DoD care.[5] For CDC care, the size of the subsidy depends on the difference between the cost to provide the care and the fees that

---

[4] The armed services use different terms to describe FCC homes, including child development homes.

[5] These differences are largely driven by the provisions of the Military Child Care Act of 1989 (MCCA). The intent of the MCCA was to improve the quality, availability, and

parents are charged. The cost to provide care varies dramatically by a child's age (Zellman and Gates, 2002), while parent fees depend on family income, not the child's age.[6] As a result, the size of the CDC subsidy is generally larger for families with younger children and/or with lower family incomes.[7]

In contrast to the high level of CDC subsidy, there is limited subsidy assistance for military families who use FCC care. Because FCC providers may set their own fees, the price charged to parents may be higher or lower than the price charged for CDC care, depending on both fee levels and family income. In general, families with lower incomes face higher fees in FCC relative to the CDC, while families in the highest-income categories may face lower fees in FCC than in the CDC. Some installations provide subsidies to FCC providers. Some subsidies help providers with general costs, such as insurance; most subsidies further specific DoD child-care goals, such as increased infant spaces, extended-hours care, and care for children with special needs. When an FCC provider claims a subsidy, she must agree to limit her fees to those charged by the CDC. Such policies obviously benefit parents and remove a disincentive for lower-income families to use FCC; however, these subsidy policies are not systematic across services. Limited subsidies for FCCs have reduced their attractiveness to

---

affordability of child care across military installations. The key lever for ensuring affordability was to require that each dollar spent by parents in CDC fees be matched by a dollar of appropriated funds (taxpayer dollars). CDC fees were to be based on total family income, with families organized into five fee categories.

6 The DoD establishes a fee schedule that defines a range of acceptable fees that may be charged by DoD CDCs. Families are divided into five income categories, and fees vary by category. For the 2004–2005 school year, allowable parent fees under the DoD fee schedule ranged from a minimum of $43 per week for families with total incomes below $28,000 per year to a maximum of $126 per week for families with total incomes over $70,000 per year. Installations in high cost-of-living areas are allowed to set slightly higher fees.

7 For example, Zellman and Gates (2002) estimate that it cost the DoD approximately $12,000 per year to provide infant care in CDCs in 1998. Parent fees for the middle-income category cover 27 percent of that cost. It cost the DoD about $6,600 to provide preschool-age care; parent fees for the middle-income category cover 53 percent of that cost. The largest subsidy is provided to parents of infants in low-income categories; the smallest subsidy goes to parents of older children in the highest-income category.

military parents and limited the value of FCC as part of the military child-care system. The flexibility that FCC care can provide in terms of hours and days of care may be underexploited because of the high price some parents face with FCC relative to CDC care.

Similarly, with a few notable exceptions, there are no subsidies available for military families who use civilian child care.[8] Because the quality of civilian child care varies dramatically, it is difficult to make general statements about the relative price of comparable-quality CDC care versus civilian child care. In the civilian sector, fees are levied consistent with the cost of care. Consequently, infant care is substantially more expensive than care for older children, where staff-to-client ratios are higher. More than 95 percent of DoD CDCs are accredited, while the rate of accreditation in the civilian sector is less than 10 percent (Campbell et al., 2000). In the civilian sector, accredited child care is typically more expensive than non-accredited child care. Therefore, while it is likely that some of the civilian child-care options available to military families are less expensive than CDC care, other accredited options are substantially more expensive, if they are available at all.[9]

Parents also express strong preferences for CDC care (Macro International, Inc., 1999; Zellman et al., 1992). Military families who prefer CDCs cite issues of cost, convenience, reliability, and safety (see Gates et al. [2006] for results from focus groups with military parents).[10] Some of that preference can be attributed to the attractive CDCs that have been built in recent years; part of the prefer-

---

[8] The DoD is providing such subsidies to some civilian providers to cover care for dependents of deployed Guard reservists while the parent is deployed. To receive the subsidy, these providers must be operating legally in the state in which they are located. In addition, DoD is subsidizing a set of providers on a more permanent basis. These providers must meet National Association for the Education of Young Children (NAEYC) accreditation standards and be operating legally in the state in which they are located.

[9] Zellman and Gates (2002) report that accredited centers that are subsidized by civilian employers levy fees that are substantially higher than the fees charged by military child-care centers. Accredited centers that are not subsidized would presumably charge even higher fees.

[10] Although, in general, military parents express preferences for CDC care, some CDC users are critical of some aspects of the CDCs, such as the fee schedule, hours of operation, and policies related to administering medicines.

ence is based in parental concerns about isolation and lack of oversight in FCCs; part of that preference is attributable to the lower level of dependability that an individual (as compared with an institution) can provide. But some part of the preference can also be explained by the fact that, for parents in the lower-fee categories, this inherently less-attractive child-care alternative also costs them more when no subsidy is provided by the DoD. As a result of these price differences, there are waiting lists for DoD CDC care on nearly all DoD installations with a CDC (U.S. Department of Defense, 2000).

The System Provides Special Preference for Dual-Military and Single-Parent Families

CDC waitlists can affect families differently, depending on family type and the age of dependent children. For example, DoD policy stipulates that the child-care system should give priority to single parents and dual-military parents. Many installations accomplish this objective by managing their CDC waitlists in such a way that priority is given to families of these types. Such policies mean that military families that include a working civilian spouse will spend substantial time on the CDC waitlist. (Families with a civilian spouse who neither works outside the home nor attends school are ineligible for full-time CDC care.) In addition, the CDC system's capacity to care for younger children (infants and pre-toddlers) is limited due to the reality of a fee policy based on family income and the fact that the cost of providing care is highest for the youngest children. To ensure adequate funding, DoD CDCs typically open far more spaces for preschool-age children than for infants. As a result, waiting lists are very long for the youngest children (Zellman and Gates, 2002) but may be nonexistent for preschool-age children; often, such spaces go begging because care for 4-year-olds or 5-year-olds can be purchased more cheaply in the community.

The DoD Child-Care Demand Formula

For 15 years, the DoD has been estimating the potential need for preschool, and separately, after-school child care using a formula that translates the basic demographic characteristics of the military population into a measure of child-care need—specifically, the number of child-care spaces required.[11] The formula was developed by military service program managers and by the OSD based on population and other demographic data from Defense Enrollment Eligibility Reporting System (DEERS) and services data. The formula was updated in 1993, 1995, 1997, and 2000 (U.S. Department of Defense, 2002). The following elements, collected at the installation level and aggregated, are included in the DoD child-care demand formula:

- Number of dependent children age 0–5 and 6–12 on each installation
- Percentage of dependent children who are part of single-parent families, dual-military families, or families with a military member and a civilian spouse
- Percentage of dependent children who live with their military parent, by family type
- Percentage of civilian spouses who work full time or part time
- Number of civilians employed on the installation.[12]

Although the formula is referred to as the "DoD child-care demand formula," it is actually a formula for determining *potential need* for child care among military families. By estimating the total number of children who require some kind of care, the child-care demand formula produces an upper bound on the potential need for DoD-sponsored child care. Because some families will choose to use non-DoD care (including parental and family care), the actual need will be less than the potential need calculated by the formula. In contrast to

---

[11] The formula, referred to as the "DoD child-care demand formula," was developed in response to the Military Child Care Act of 1989, which required the Department of Defense to submit a report outlining the expected child-care demand over a five-year period, from fiscal year 1991 through 1995, and a plan for meeting the demand, including the cost of implementation.

[12] The children of DoD civilian personnel who work on an installation are eligible for care in the DoD CDCs, and the child-care demand formula accounts for the potential need on the part of such families. Our study focuses on military families only.

child-care need, child-care *demand* is a more complex concept that is difficult to measure.[13]

As an employer of many individuals with dependent children who must relocate to do their work, the DoD is much more concerned than are most U.S. employers with meeting their employees' child-care needs. The military has a keen interest in ensuring that parents who need some form of child care in order to show up for work every day receive that care and that the quality of the care received is high enough that parents do not worry about their children and can focus their attention on their work.[14] These parents may or may not use DoD-sponsored care, and they may or may not be satisfied with the care they are using.

DoD reports that describe the formula acknowledge that many factors other than demographic characteristics may increase or decrease child-care need, including force reduction, deployments, base closure, quality improvements, and cost of DoD-provided care. In addition, the cost, quality, and availability of care in the community surrounding an installation affect the need for DoD-sponsored child care (Jehn, 1990; Office of the Secretary of Defense, Force Management and Personnel, 1992). Each of the four military services has taken the DoD formula and applied it at the installation level to take into account these specific factors (see Appendix A for a detailed description of the application of the formula by each of the services).

Objectives

The primary purpose of this study is to assess the validity of the DoD formula as a tool for translating information on military families into measures of potential child-care need and to suggest ways that the tool

---

[13] See Gates et al. (2006) for a more detailed discussion of child-care demand and the study's methodology and major findings.

[14] According to a 2003 study by the Bureau of Labor Statistics, 5 percent of U.S. civilian employers provide on-site or near-site child care, and 3 percent provide a subsidy for child care. Ten percent of employers provide services to help employees find care (Kiger, 2004).

might be improved. A secondary purpose is to clarify understanding of the indicators that influence key child-care outcomes. A third is to examine the formula more broadly in terms of its contributions to identifying and prioritizing DoD goals for military child care. In this report, we compare the parameters and assumptions of the DoD formula with data collected in 2004 through a nationwide survey of military families who were asked about their use of child care. We address how well the current data source for the formula reflects the demographic characteristics of military families and what might be done to improve the accuracy of information on which the formula relies. We also examine how well the current DoD formula predicts potential need and how the DoD might better translate potential need into a measure of the number and type of spaces required by military families.

Measures of Child-Care Need

There are a number of ways to think about and measure the extent to which the DoD is meeting the child-care needs of military families. In this section, we define the key intermediate and final outcomes that we use in our analyses. Each of the measures provides a different perspective on the need for child care and the role of DoD in meeting that need.

Ultimately, the DoD child-care system must be assessed in terms of the support it provides to military outcomes. Therefore, we focus on two final outcome measures: readiness of military members and the likelihood of leaving the military due to child-care issues. These intermediate outcomes (child-care use, unmet need for care, and unmet preference for care) are posited to influence readiness and retention.

These terms and others that are used frequently in this report are defined below. Specialized meanings unique to this report are discussed in more detail following a brief generic definition.

In defining these terms, we make a distinction between families who use formal child-care arrangements and those who use an informal arrangement. We consider an arrangement to be a *formal arrangement* if it involves providers other than friends or family members and occurs on a regular basis during working hours. Formal child-care arrangements for military families may include DoD-sponsored centers or FCC homes and the full range of options available to non-military parents, including off-base centers, civilian FCC, and nannies. *Informal arrangements* include care provided by siblings, relatives or friends, and the child himself.[15] Parental care is a third option that falls into neither category.

We recognize that not all families want to use formal child-care arrangements. Indeed, some parents make significant sacrifices, such as requesting work on alternate shifts, to ensure that they can care for their children themselves, even if each parent works full time. Another important category of non-users of child care includes parents who are able to support one of them staying at home, either to exclusively care for children or to combine work at home with child care.

Child-Care Use

Child-care use refers to the care that a given family actually uses at a given point in time. It may be at one care setting or several. While use ideally reflects preference, depending on location, income, and needs, some families use child care that is quite different from the care they might prefer. We examine *child-care use* as an intermediate outcome of interest. Although child-care use is not a measure of need, our examination of child-care use allows us to describe the extent to which those who are using some form of child care are being served by the DoD system.

Unmet Need for Care

Unmet need for care refers to a situation in which a family reports that it does not have sufficient child care to meet its duty and other obligations. In defining and analyzing unmet need, we consider the parents' perspective and define unmet need to exist when parents report that

---

[15] DoD regulations prohibit self-care by children age 12 and under. However, we asked about such care in the families we surveyed (all of whom had a child 12 and under) because we believed that self-care does occur among younger children, and we needed to understand its frequency and the circumstances under which it occurs. Assurances of confidentiality were offered to parents to encourage them to reveal such arrangements.

they would like to use a formal child-care arrangement but are not currently doing so. This category might include parents who care for their children themselves and parents who rely on friends, older siblings, or other relatives for child care. One might question our focus on such a broad definition of unmet need. In fact, we considered several possible definitions of unmet need, including a focus on families who report that a lack of child-care options prevents a parent from working outside the home and a focus on parents who use parental, sibling, or self-care, but these more-restrictive definitions captured very few families among our survey respondents.

Unmet Preference

In contrast to unmet need, families with *unmet preference* are able to meet their obligations with the child care they have but would prefer to use another arrangement. As noted above, the military subsidizes CDCs quite heavily. In contrast, FCC homes are subsidized at a much lower level, and sometimes not at all. Other choices are not subsidized. In addition, CDCs are generally viewed as both safer and more reliable. Consequently, there may be a substantial unmet preference for CDCs. Many parents are unable to get their children into CDCs and make other arrangements that turn out to be acceptable, even desirable, over time. But many parents maintain a preference for CDC care. While we are not arguing that DoD should strive to provide each family with its most preferred form of child care, monitoring unmet preference may help DoD ensure that it is not devoting resources to a type of care that families do not want to use.

Child Care and Military Readiness

Child care and military readiness refers to a relationship that has been demonstrated to exist between the availability and quality of child care and the ability of parents to both appear on time for duty and to be able to focus on work while they are at work. If child care is not available, a parent is likely to need to stay home; if the quality of care is low, parents are likely to be worrying about their children's welfare and not focusing on work. Military readiness, or whether child-care issues keep parents from reporting for military duty or cause them to be late or miss work as a result of child-care issues, is one of our two key outcome measures.

Likelihood of Leaving the Military Due to Child-Care Issues

The *likelihood of leaving the military due to child-care issues* refers to the behavioral intentions of active duty members and their families concerning separating from the military. Because surveys can assess only behavioral intentions, this is not an actual behavior. However, the psychological literature generally finds that behavioral intentions are a reasonably good predictor of behavior. Propensity to leave may be driven by many factors; we focus on those individuals who report that they intend to leave the military because of child-care issues. Note that some families who report a propensity to leave due to child-care issues may be "served" by the system in the sense that they have an arrangement (even a DoD-sponsored arrangement) that they use. Nevertheless, some aspects of their child-care arrangements are inadequate to the point of propelling them to leave the military.

The DoD Formula and Child-Care Outcomes

As the discussion in this chapter suggests, the policy environment related to DoD's child-care demand formula is a complicated one. Figure 1.1 illustrates the important distinction between potential need as calculated by the DoD formula and the key child-care outcomes of interest.[16] As discussed earlier, the DoD formula translates information about military families with children under 13 years of age into a measure of the potential need for child care (i.e., the number of dependent children who might need some form of non-parental child care). But this measure tells DoD relatively little about the number, type, and location of child-care spaces needed to maximize military readiness and retention. Family characteristics, including the child-care choices

---

[16] *Wraparound care* (under "possible policy responses" in the figure) is child care that is provided before a CDC or FCC opens for the day and after it closes. CDCs and FCC typically have standard hours of operation, but military families often have workdays (or have to work 24-hour shifts) that extend beyond the hours of operation.

Figure 1.1
Family, Installation, and Policy Characteristics that Affect Child-Care Outcomes

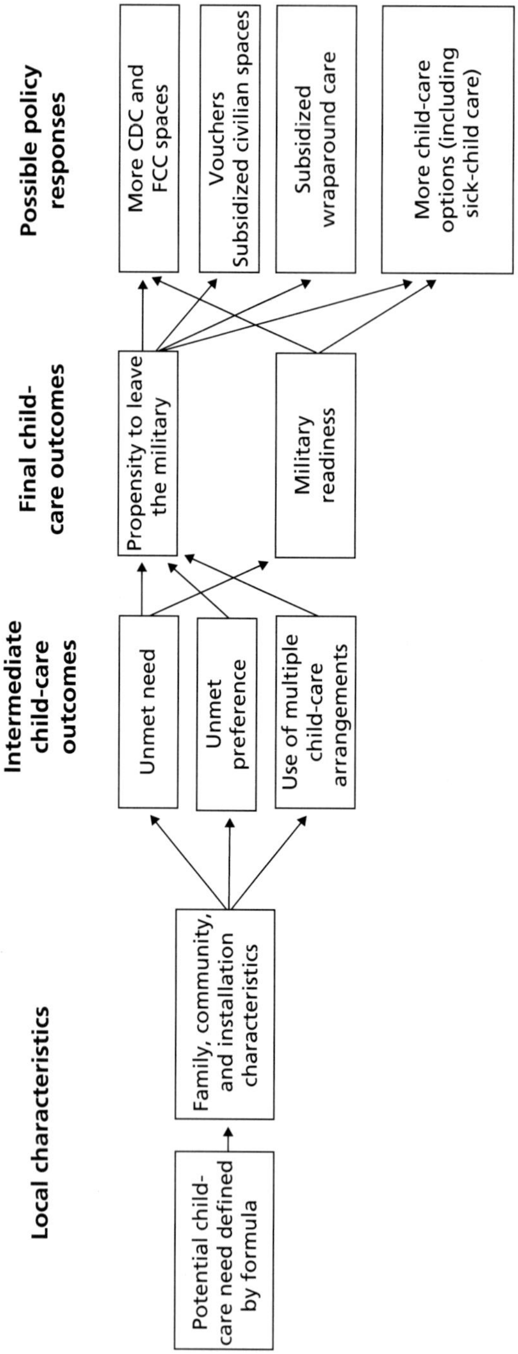

RAND *MG387-1.1*

that families make, and installation characteristics impact the extent to which this potential need translates into the "intermediate child-care outcomes" of unmet child-care need, unmet child-care preference, and the use of multiple child-care arrangements. These intermediate outcomes can, in turn, influence the outcomes of greatest interest to DoD: military readiness and propensity to leave the military. Although not all intermediate outcomes are expected to influence each final outcome for each family, we expect that indications of substantial unmet need, unmet preference, and use of multiple care arrangements will translate into lower levels of military readiness and greater propensity to leave the military. A variety of policy options is available to DoD to improve readiness and retention through child-care policy. The most effective policy option will likely depend on the final outcome and the intermediate outcomes that most affect that final outcome being addressed.

Methodology

Our analyses are based on information gathered through a survey of military families with dependent children between the ages of 0 and 12. The survey was fielded between February and August 2004. The sample, drawn by the Defense Manpower Data Center (DMDC) from DEERS data, includes families of active duty military members, including activated reservists, stationed in the United States. Although being stationed in the United States was a criterion for being included in the survey sample, the military member may have been deployed abroad at the time of the survey. Surveys were sent to home mailing addresses and could be completed by a military parent or civilian spouse.

The sample frame included all military members who reported having dependent children age 12 or younger as of September 2003. We used information from the DEERS file to determine whether the military member is a single parent, the family is dual military, or the family has two adults, only one of whom is in the military. Using a clustered sample design, we sampled survey participants by indicated family type and asked them to describe child care for a randomly selected target child. Our survey sample included 3,000 military families. We received 1,137 responses to the survey, for a response rate of 34 percent. Of the 1,137 survey responses, 109, or 10 percent, responded that the target child (the child inquired about in the survey) did not live with them and they had no input into the child-care decisions for that child. Thus, our final analytic sample for the survey numbers 1,028. Table 1.1 provides a breakdown of the number of responses by child age, family type, and service.

The survey covered a wide range of issues related to child-care need, including current child-care arrangements, reasons for choice of those arrangements, and the relationship between child care on the one hand and military readiness and retention on the other. The survey asked questions about the most recent deployment of a military member and how that influenced the need for child care. The survey also asked about family characteristics, such as family status, spouse employment status, and distance between home and base, among others, so that we might understand how those characteristics influence child-care choices and career choices. As we note later in this report, the description of family type based on information from the DEERS file differed in many cases from the reported family type for many survey respondents.[17]

Table 1.1
Number of Survey Respondents, by Child Age, Family Type, and Service

Child Age and Service	Single Parent	Dual Military	Civilian Spouse
Child age 0–5	58	241	164
Child age 6–12	53	161	198
Army	36	57	133
Navy	36	34	136
Air Force	46	361	136
Marines	6	3	36
Total [a]	124	455	439

[a] Total includes families for which the child age was missing or the target child was over the age of 12.

[17] For a more detailed description of the survey and methodology, see Gates et al. (2006).

The survey content was informed by a series of focus group meetings with military parents. We conducted 21 focus groups at eight installations across the country from November 2002 through July 2003. We visited two installations from each service. Focus group participants included mothers and fathers; in most cases, the participating parent was a military member. Participants represented single-parent and dual-military families and families with a civilian spouse.

In this report, we present tabulations of the survey results in order to provide a descriptive overview of child-care use, unmet child-care need, unmet child-care preference, the impact of child-care issues on military readiness, and retention intentions. Unless otherwise noted, these descriptive tabulations are based on weighted survey data. The weighting methodology, described in detail in Gates et al. (2006), is required to produce results that are representative of the military population stationed in the United States. The weighting accounts for both a stratified sample design[18] and differences in response rates by military service, rank, race, education level, and gender.[19]

This report also summarizes the key results of multivariate analyses of the child-care survey data. These analyses, presented in Gates et al. (2006), use bivariate and multivariate logit models to examine the relationship between family and installation characteristics and the three intermediate and two final child-care outcomes: (1) the type of

---

[18] The stratified sample design is used to ensure that the survey population captured a reasonable number of dual-military and single-parent families. The six strata, described earlier, are based on the age of the child (0–5 years and 6–12 years) and family status (single parent, dual-military parents, or a military parent married to a civilian). We sampled 500 families from each of the six strata. Because the survey asks families about the child-care arrangement for only one randomly selected "target" child, weights are constructed at the family level.

[19] We use a logit model to estimate the probability that a response to the survey was a function of certain characteristics of the sampled population and to construct the non-response weights. The analysis reveals that women are substantially more likely than men to respond to the survey, as are more highly educated individuals. Blacks are less likely than whites to respond. Individuals in the Army are less likely than those in the Air Force to respond. Officers and senior enlisted personnel are more likely to respond to the survey than junior-level officers and enlisted personnel.

care used by the family, (2) unmet need, (3) unmet preference, (4) time lost to duty because of child-care problems, and (5) the propensity to leave the military due to child-care issues.

Organization of This Monograph

In Chapter Two, we provide an overview of the assumptions of the DoD child-care demand formula. In Chapter Three, we compare the assumptions built into the DoD demand formula with the descriptive statistics from the survey data to see how well the formula's assumptions hold among respondents to our survey. In Chapter Four, we provide an overview and analysis of our child-care survey responses, highlighting the types of care used by military families and examining unmet need and preference reported by parents. In Chapter Five, we present conclusions based on these data and recommendations about how DoD might better use the formula to meet the goals of the DoD child-care system. Appendix A provides a detailed description of the components of the DoD child-care demand formula. Appendix B contains the military child-care survey form.

CHAPTER TWO

Examining DoD Child-Care Demand Formula Assumptions

In this chapter, we describe the assumptions underlying the current DoD child-care demand formula. This information will inform our assessment of the formula's accuracy and our discussion of how the formula might be altered to improve its usefulness to the DoD.

Data

The DoD child-care demand formula is used to estimate the number of children of military families who potentially need child care in some form. The formula relies on data obtained from the DMDC's DEERS file, which contains information on all military members and their dependents; these data enable the DoD to identify the number of dependent children age 0–12 and to calculate the percentage of those children who are part of single-parent families, dual-military families, and families with a military parent married to a civilian. These data provide the starting point for the formula calculation.

The DEERS data file is a central repository of information on military families and includes five categories of information:

- Personal: Social Security number, date of birth, sex, marital status, number of dependents
- Personnel: organization, pay grade, occupation
- Service-related: service, unit identification code

- Benefits: eligibility status for medical, dental, and education benefits
- Geographic: address, state, zip code.

While the information in some of these categories is updated in the DEERS database through the various uniformed service personnel systems on a daily, monthly, or other periodic basis, personal information is designed to be submitted and updated in the DEERS file immediately through the Real-Time Automated Personnel Identification Card System (RAPIDS). A military member is responsible for updating all changes to his or her family status, including a change in marital status or number of dependents, within 30 days of the event.

Assumptions

The child-care demand formula uses DMDC DEERS data on the number of dependent children of military members as the starting point for its calculation of potential child-care need. It then makes assumptions using historical information from DEERS about how many of those dependent children are part of different family "types," including single-parent, dual-military, and military-married-to-civilian families, and how many of these dependent children are living with their parents. It also makes assumptions about how many have a civilian parent working, based on information from the services.

Tables 2.1 and 2.2 summarize the DoD formula and the percentages used to calculate the *potential need* for child care among 0- to 5-year-olds and 6- to 12-year-olds. For children age 0–5, the formula assumes that 8 percent of dependent children are part of single-parent families, 4 percent are part of dual-military families, and 88 percent are part of military families with a civilian spouse. The formula also assumes that 85 percent of the children of dual-military families live with their parents and that 90 percent of other dependent children also do so (see Table 2.1). With respect to military families that include a civilian spouse, the formula assumes that 43 percent of spouses work outside the home and that 60 percent of those working spouses work full time (see Table 2.1). Finally, the formula assumes that a family with a civilian spouse who works part time requires half-time child care (see Table 2.1). The formula for children age 6–12 is similar to that for children age 0–5, although it assumes that a higher fraction of civilian spouses with children in that age range are working (58 percent) and that a greater proportion of working spouses are working full time (65 percent) (see Table 2.2).[1]

Table 2.1
DoD Child-Care Demand Formula for Children Age 0–5

Categories of Child-Care Users	Assumptions
(1) Children age 0–5	—
(2) Children of single parents [a]	(1) × 0.08 × 0.90
(3) Children of dual-military couples [b]	(1) × 0.04 × 0.85
(4) Children of military married to civilians [c]	(1) × 0.88 × 0.90
(5) Children of spouses working full time [d]	(4) × 0.43 × 0.60
(6) Children of spouses working part time [e]	(4) × 0.43 × 0.40 × 0.50
(7) Civilian need for child-care spaces	Total number of civilians × 0.0125 [f]
(8) Total number of spaces needed	(2) + (3) + (5) + (6) + (7)

[a] Number of children age 0–5 × percentage of children age 0–5 of single parents × percentage living with their parents.

[b] Number of children age 0–5 × percentage of children age 0–5 of dual-military couples × percentage of children living with their parents.

[c] Number of children age 0–5 × percentage of children age 0–5 of military married to civilians x percentage of children living with their parents.

[d] Number of children of military married to civilians × percentage with second parent employed outside the home × percentage employed full time (note: for all except the Navy).

[e] Number of children of military married to civilians × percentage of children of single parents × percentage employed part time × 1/2 space for each (note: for all except the Navy).

[f] Although they have lower priority on waitlists, the children of DoD civil service employees are eligible for care in DoD CDCs and DoD FCC. This formula generates a rough estimate of the need for care by DoD civil service employees and reflects an assumption that 1.25 percent of civil service employees will need child care.

---

[1] Although we use the term "assumptions" to describe the formula's components throughout this report, the formula is actually based on historical data from the DMDC DEERS data file, as described in Chapter One.

Table 2.2
DoD Child-Care Demand Formula for Children Age 6–12

Categories of Child-Care Users	Assumptions
(1) Children age 6–12	—
(2) Children of single parents	(1) × 0.08 × 0.90
(3) Children of dual-military couples	(1) × 0.04 × 0.85
(4) Children of military married to civilians	(1) × 0.88 × 0.90
(5) Children of spouses working full time	(4) × 0.58 × 0.65
(6) Children of spouses working part time	(4) × 0.58 × 0.35 × 0.50
(7) Civilian need for child-care spaces	Total number of civilians × 0.0125
(8) Total number of spaces needed	(2) + (3) + (5) + (6) + (7) × 33 percent

As discussed above, this formula translates basic demographic data on military families into potential child-care need. The number generated by the formula will represent the upper bound on the amount of care that will be needed by military families, since not all families will want DoD care.

Factors Not Included in Formula

Various factors will increase or decrease the overall need for care on a given installation, including the number and grade of military and civilians assigned to that installation, the percentage of military population living on the installation, the mission of the installation and the need for shift work, and the amount and type of care provided in the local area. The influence of these factors is acknowledged in some DoD reports. It is also acknowledged that not all parents will want or need care provided by the DoD, since, as stated in an OSD report, "many of these children are currently cared for in other civilian resources or through relative care" (Office of the Secretary of Defense, Force Management and Personnel, 1992, p. 11). However, the DoD does not formally take these factors into account in translating potential need, as defined by the formula, into an estimate closer to the actual number of child-care spaces required by the DoD system.

The number of spaces generated by the formula is then considered in light of available resources and competing demands to arrive at a goal for the amount of child care that the DoD system should provide. The approach used by the DoD to translate potential need, as specified by the formula, into the amount of child care or number of spaces the system should provide has always been subject to changing political influences at the DoD level, including resource availability and concerns with readiness and retention.

Issues Examined in This Study

The ultimate question of interest for this study is how closely the number of spaces DoD establishes as its goal matches the actual number of DoD-sponsored child-care spaces required to effectively meet the needs of military families. As noted above, DoD's target number may be influenced by the accuracy of the formula itself in terms of estimating the *potential need* for care. The target number may also be influenced by the process of considering that estimate of potential need against other concerns in coming up with a concrete goal for the number of spaces to provide. The following chapters address the accuracy of the current formula in estimating potential need, how the formula might be supplemented with other information to better determine the need for child care among military families, and what policies might help DoD to better meet that need.

CHAPTER THREE

Accuracy of the DoD Child-Care Formula Estimate

In this chapter, we explore how accurately the child-care demand formula predicts the number of child-care spaces that are required to support the child-care need of military families. In doing so, we consider three issues: the accuracy of the DEERS data regarding family status, the validity of the assumptions included in the formula about the propensity of minor dependents to live with their parents, and the percentage of civilian spouses who work or attend school outside the home.

As described in the preceding chapter, the formula makes different assumptions about the need for child care among different types of families; therefore, it is important to consider the accuracy of the assumptions that are used to calculate children's family types.

Accuracy of Family Status Indicators in DEERS Data

We examined the extent to which family status reported by our survey respondents corresponded to the expected family status based on information in the DEERS data.[1] As discussed in the preceding chapter, the DEERS data are used by DoD in defining parameters for the child-care demand formula. Therefore, the accuracy of the data on which the

[1] Throughout this report, we refer to parents with respect to their relationship to a single randomly selected target child, but we recognize that many parents have additional children, both in the same age range and in the other age ranges. In our analyses, we first controlled for the presence of additional children. When we found no effects of the "other children" variable on analytic results, the variable was dropped.

DoD demand formula is based at a given point in time is an important aspect of how effective the formula can be in estimating potential child-care need.

Our analysis of the survey results revealed a high level of mismatch between the expected family type based on DEERS data and the family type reported in survey responses. To describe these results, we present figures showing the reported family type for individuals that we "predicted" would be part of single-parent, dual-military, or civilian-spouse families based on DEERS data.

Figure 3.1 indicates that among families with children age 0–5 who were identified by DEERS data as single-parent families, 43 percent identified themselves as single-parent families on the survey. Fifty-seven percent of families identified as single-parent families in the DEERS data defined themselves differently on the survey: 6 percent reported dual-military family status, and 51 percent stated that their family status is military member married to a civilian.[2, 3]

Figure 3.1 also reveals that among families with children age 0–5 identified in the DEERS data file as having dual-military status, 89 percent reported dual-military status on the survey. Two percent reported single-parent status, and 9 percent reported their family status as military member married to a civilian.[4]

Similar results were found for families with children age 0–5 identified by the DEERS data file to be families with military members who were married to civilians. Eighty-one percent of those families reported military-married-to-civilian status on the survey. Eight

---

2 Two percent of those in the sample did not state their marital status.

3 The single-family charts reflect the point estimates based on weighted survey responses. Confidence intervals around this estimate suggest that, with 95-percent probability, the fraction of single parents, as identified in the DMDC database, reporting single-parent status in the survey is between 32 percent and 54 percent.

4 The dual-military charts reflect the point estimates based on weighted survey responses. Confidence intervals around this estimate suggest that, with 95-percent probability, the fraction of dual-military parents, as identified in the DMDC database, reporting dual-military parent status in the survey is between 83 percent and 93 percent.

percent reported single-parent status, and 11 percent reported dual-military status.[5]

Figure 3.1
Family Status Reported in RAND Child-Care Survey for Families Identified in the DEERS Data File

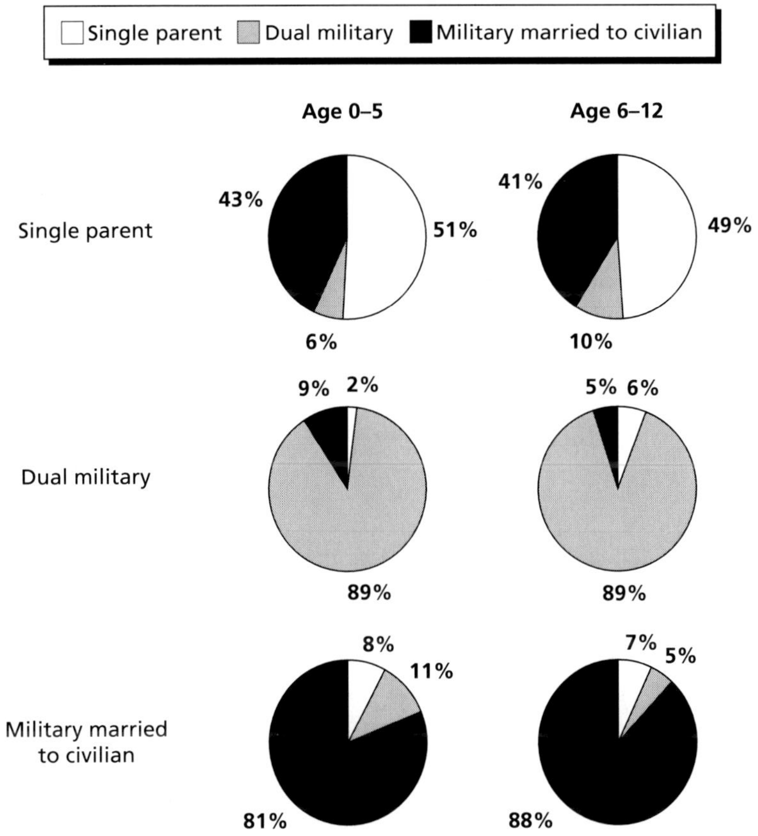

RAND *MG387-3.1*

5 The military-married-to-civilian chart reflects the point estimates based on weighted survey responses. Confidence intervals around this estimate suggest that, with 95-percent probability, the fraction of military-married-to-civilian parents, as identified in the DMDC database, reporting military-married-to-civilian parent status in the survey is between 71 percent and 88 percent.

Similarly, 49 percent of those with a child between the age of 6 and 12 who were identified as a single parent in the DEERS data reported the same family status in the survey,[6] while 41 percent identified their family status as military member married to a civilian, and 10 percent reported dual-military family status. Of families that were identified as dual military in the DEERS data, 89 percent reported the same status on the survey,[7] while 6 percent reported single-parent family status, and 5 percent were military-married-to-civilian families. Similarly, 88 percent of military-married-to-civilian families identified in the DEERS data reported the same status in the survey,[8] while 7 percent reported single-parent status, and 5 percent reported dual-military status.

Implications

These deviations between family status indicated by the DEERS data and family status reported on the survey, which are substantiated in some categories, suggest that relying on DEERS data for accurate information on the family status of military families may be problematic. This is particularly true for military members who appear to be single parents in the DEERS data. The differences suggest that family status is quite dynamic, especially for single-parent families. It appears that there is significant movement from single-parent status to military-member-married-to-civilian status, and vice versa. The time lag between when data are collected by DMDC and when current child-care need projections are made should be considered in the application of the formula; more research is needed to clarify just how

---

[6] Confidence intervals around this estimate suggest that, with 95-percent probability, the fraction of single-parent families, as identified in the DMDC database, reporting single-parent status in the survey is between 36 percent and 61 percent.

[7] Confidence intervals around this estimate suggest that, with 95-percent probability, the fraction of dual-military families, as identified in the DMDC database, reporting dual-military status in the survey is between 78 percent and 94 percent.

[8] Confidence intervals around this estimate suggest that, with 95-percent probability, the fraction of military-married-to-civilian families, as identified in the DMDC database, reporting military-married-to-civilian parent status in the survey is between 81 percent and 93 percent.

dynamic these family statuses are. Certainly, the dynamic nature of family status needs to be considered by policymakers when utilizing the child-care demand formula. Misclassification of military-married-to-civilian families as single-parent or dual-military families (or vice versa) is important to the estimation of child-care demand because the demand formula assumes that single-parent and dual-military families are much more likely to need child care.

It is possible that some of the deviation may have resulted from a failure on the part of military members to update their family status in DEERS. Incentives to update family status vary. Some changes, such as the birth of a child or marriage, will result in an increase in benefits, while other changes, such as divorce, will mean a decrease in benefits. Thus, it is possible that some members intentionally delay updating their information. Others, no doubt, are simply too busy and distracted by their many responsibilities to do the updating. Another problem encountered in tracking family status in the DMDC data is the lack of a dual-military family flag. Although this flag used to be contained in the DMDC data, it is no longer recorded in the DoD-wide DEERS database.[9] This makes it very difficult to determine the size of this group of important DoD child-care consumers.

Fraction of Children Who Live with Their Parents

As shown in Table 3.1, compared with the assumptions of the current DoD demand formula, the survey responses suggest that, among

---

[9] Although we had been informed by officials at DMDC that it is possible to identify dual-military spouses, when we obtained the data, we discovered that the DEERS file no longer includes a dual-military flag. Because it was important to survey dual-military families, and only a small number of such families would be reached through a random sample of military families, we asked DMDC to construct a dual-military identifier by looking for active duty service members who report spouses who are also active duty service members (we looked for unique identifiers that identify individuals as both sponsors [military members with a dependent spouse] and their dependent spouses). Through this method, we identified approximately 10,000 dual-military families, which is about one-third of what we expected based on a comparison with other data sources.

Table 3.1
Comparison of DoD Formula and RAND Child-Care Survey: Percentage of Children Living with Their Parents

	DoD Formula [a]	RAND Child-Care Survey, Children Age 0–5 (confidence intervals)	RAND Child-Care Survey, Children Age 6–12 (confidence intervals)
Children in single-parent families living with their parent	90	69 (48, 85)	72 (58, 83)
Children in dual-military families living with their parents	85	99 (99, 100)	99 (98, 100)
Children in military-married-to-civilian families living with their parents	90	89 (78, 95)	79 (71, 85)

[a] The DoD formula assumptions are the same for children age 0–5 and children age 6–12.

NOTE: The 95-percent confidence intervals around the point estimates are based on weighted survey data.

families with children age 0–5, more children of dual-military families live with their parents, and fewer children of single parents live with a single military parent.[10] The DoD formula posits that 85 percent of children of dual-military families live with their parents, but our survey reveals that approximately 99 percent of those children are living with their parents. The formula assumes that 90 percent of children age 0–5 with a single military parent are living with that parent; in contrast, our survey results show that 69 percent are living with that parent. The survey data indicate that the number of children living with their parents in families with a military member married to a civilian spouse closely matches what is assumed in the formula; 89 percent were found to be living with their parents according to our survey data, compared with 90 percent specified in the formula.

A comparison of the DoD demand formula assumptions and our survey data for 6- to 12-year-olds reveals results similar to those for

[10] The reported survey results include responses from parents who returned a blank survey because their child does not live with them. We included these respondents in the calculation to more accurately capture the universe of families.

families with children age 0–5 (see Table 3.1). The percentage of children age 6–12 living with dual-military parents is 99 percent among survey respondents, compared with 85 percent estimated in the formula. The percentage is lower for children living with their parents in families with a military member married to a civilian. Seventy-nine percent of the respondents report military-married-to-civilian status in the survey, whereas the formula assumes 90 percent of children of this family type live with their parents. Finally, the percentage of children in single-parent families who live with that parent is 72 percent among the survey population compared with 90 percent estimated in the formula.

Implications

Overestimation and underestimation of the number of children living with a military parent are likely to affect the accuracy of projections of potential child-care need. Underestimating the number of children living with dual-military parents, and overestimating the number in the case of single parents with children age 0–5 and military members married to civilian families with both preschool-age and school-age children, will produce distorted estimates of potential need for child care.

Fraction of Civilian Spouses Who Work or Attend School

Other DoD child-care demand formula assumptions also differed from the distributions found among survey respondents. Our data show that the proportion of civilian spouses of military members working outside the home or attending school is approximately 10 percent less than what the formula assumes for families with children age 0–5. The percentage of civilian spouses working full time is 20 points higher among our survey respondents than the percentage assumed in the formula, and the percentage of civilian spouses engaging in part-time work is about 20 points lower among our survey respondents than that assumed in the formula. Table 3.2 compares the percentage of civilian spouses working outside the home in our survey population and in the DoD demand formula.[11]

A dramatic divergence was found in the percentage of civilian spouses working outside the home or attending school in families with children age 6–12. The percentage is 14 points lower among our survey population than the percentage in the formula.[12] There is no statistically significant difference between the relative proportion of part-time and full-time employment among working civilians between our survey population and the formula (see Table 3.2).

Implications

These results suggest that the DoD formula assumptions about employment patterns of civilian spouses may need to be revisited. Civilian

Table 3.2
Comparison of DoD Formula and RAND Child-Care Survey: Percentage of Civilian Spouses Working Outside the Home

	DoD Formula, for Children Age 0–5	RAND Child-Care Survey, Families with Children Age 0–5 (confidence intervals)	DoD Formula, for Children Age 6–12	RAND Child-Care Survey, Families with Children Age 6–12 (confidence intervals)
Civilian spouses working outside the home	43	33 (24, 44)	58	44 (35, 52)
Civilian spouses working full time	60	80 (66, 89)	65	75 (63, 85)
Civilian spouses working part time	40	20 (11, 34)	35	28 (18, 40)

NOTE: The 95-percent confidence intervals around the point estimates are based on weighted survey data.

---

[11] As noted above, the response rate for the survey was low (34 percent), creating the possibility of non-response bias. To account for this possibility, weights were created and applied to these statistics. For more information on the non-response analysis, see Gates et al. (2006).

[12] Hosek et al. (2002) found that the probability of working outside the home declines with age for the civilian wives of military members. Such a decline is not evident in the civilian population as a whole.

parents of children age 0–5 appear to be working outside the home slightly less than what the DoD formula assumes, but of those who are working, full-time employment is relatively more common. Based on the formula assumptions, the fraction of civilian parents of children age 6–12 who work outside the home appears to be high compared with the percentage from our survey data. These findings have important implications for the amount and type of care these families need. DoD may want to further explore these discrepancies to ensure that the child-care needs of these families are accurately represented as a component of the potential child-care needs of military families.

Conclusion

The data presented in this chapter point to several areas in which the assumptions used in the DoD formula differ from the responses to our survey. DoD may want to examine these discrepancies to determine whether they call for changes to the DoD formula.

It should be noted that the low survey response rate (34 percent) may account for some portion of the substantial differences between the family-status distributions in the DEERS data and those reported by our survey respondents. To account for non-response bias, weights were developed and applied in reporting and analyzing the results of the survey. In constructing the weights, we were limited to data elements that were available in the DEERS data file that was used to select the sample. Although the use of weighted data increases the standard error of our point estimates, we still find statistically significant differences between the formula parameters and the survey responses. Nevertheless, readers should be cautioned that our point estimates may be biased if the weighting strategy did not fully account for non-response bias.

CHAPTER FOUR

Evaluating How the Current Child-Care System Is Serving Military Families

As described in the preceding chapters, the DoD child-care demand formula provides a measure of the *potential* need for child care among military families, but potential need overestimates *actual* need. An important policy question is how potential need relates to child-care outcomes of interest, in particular, military members' readiness and retention, and the extent to which policy levers can influence that relationship. Traditionally, the key policy lever used by the DoD to impact need has been the number of DoD-sponsored child-care spaces available in the system. Indeed, in the past, the DoD has been committed to meeting some percentage of potential need calculated by the formula by providing a designated number of spaces. However, there may be other policy levers that could have as much or more impact on key readiness and retention outcomes. DoD needs richer knowledge of how the system works to consider the relationship between various policy levers and readiness and retention.

DoD has long recognized that it recruits individuals but it retains families. This notion reflects the fact that, if a military member's family is not happy with the military lifestyle, then that member is likely to leave the military. Recent RAND research suggests that military families with employed civilian spouses tend to be more satisfied with military life (Harrell et al., 2004). Other RAND research reveals that civilian wives of military members are less likely to work outside the home, and when they do work outside the home, they earn less than their counterparts with non-military husbands. Their lower wages are due to a combination of fewer weeks of work per year and lower hourly wages

(Hosek et al., 2002). In interviews, a substantial number of spouses of military members cited child-care problems as a reason for not seeking work outside the home (Harrell et al., 2004).

In this chapter, we examine how the child-care system is currently being used and the extent to which parents report that it is meeting their needs. We discuss the results from the RAND child-care survey and what those results say about the following child-care–related outcomes: child-care use, unmet child-care need, unmet child-care preference, readiness of military members, and the likelihood of personnel leaving the military due to child-care issues. The intent of this analysis is to explore the extent to which families with children who need care are using the DoD system and to identify family and installation characteristics that relate to various measures of child-care use and need. These analyses will help DoD to better understand the output of its child-care demand formula and develop goals for addressing the child-care needs of military families.[1]

Child-Care Use

Although child-care use is not a measure of need, information about child-care use allows us to describe the extent to which those who are using some form of child care are being served by the DoD system. In this section, we describe the survey findings concerning patterns of child-care use for the various family types and provide information about the reasons why certain child-care options were chosen.

Single-Parent Families

As shown in Table 4.1, among single parents of children age 0–5, DoD CDCs appear to be the most popular form of care (with 24 percent of children), followed closely by civilian child-care centers (21 percent). In contrast, DoD FCC and civilian FCC are used by only a small fraction (5 percent) of single parents.

---

[1] For a detailed description of the data and methodology on which these analyses are based, see Gates et al. (2006).

Table 4.1
Percentage of Children Age 0–5 in Each Child-Care Arrangement, by Family Type

Arrangement	Single Parent	Dual Military	Civilian Spouse
DoD CDC	24	42	11
DoD FCC	5	10	11
DoD youth center	8	0	0
Civilian after-school program	< 1	< 1	< 1
Civilian child-care center	21	13	12
Civilian FCC	5	12	2
Relative	5	7	4
Mother	21	< 1	41
Father	0	0	< 1
Sibling	0	0	0
Self-care	< 1	0	< 1
Non-relative	7	13	4
Other or missing	5	2	12
Number of observations	58	241	162

The popularity of CDC care among parents in this group may be due to the enrollment preference that single parents receive, as well as to the low fees levied on families with the lowest incomes. Indeed, single parents reported availability and cost as the most important reasons for selecting this type of care. Civilian care may be a preferred option because it is less expensive than FCC or even subsidized DoD CDC care in some areas. Parents using civilian child-care centers cited hours of operation and cost as the most important reasons for selecting this type of care.

Nearly 21 percent of single parents with children age 0–5 reported that care provided by the mother of the children is the primary care arrangement, a figure that at first seems surprisingly high in a group of single military members. But analysis revealed that all the single parents who reported the mother as the primary caregiver were male military members. It is possible that the children of these families are cared for by their mothers in a location near where the military members live, or that the mother and father are cohabiting but are not married. Seven percent of single-parent families reported the use of a non-relative in or outside the home as the primary care arrangement. Findings concerning use of a non-relative as the primary caregiver suggest that many single parents rely on an informal network of friends and babysitters to meet their need for child care.

Table 4.2 shows child-care usage rates among single-parent families with children age 6–12. The most common primary child-care arrangement among this group is care provided by the mother (41 percent). As is the case in families with younger children, almost all (99 percent) of these single parents are male. These single parents cited quality of care as the most important reason for choosing maternal care as their primary child-care arrangement. After-school programs are used by many single-parent families with children age 6–12, with

Table 4.2
Percentage of Children Age 6–12 in Each Child-Care Arrangement, by Family Type

Arrangement	Single Parent	Dual Military	Civilian Spouse
DoD CDC	4	< 1	1
DoD FCC	0	< 1	1
DoD school-age care (SAC) [a]	4	3	1
DoD youth center	4	4	4
DoD after-school program	2	13	2
Civilian after-school program	14	61	5
Civilian child-care center	3	< 1	4
Civilian FCC	2	3	< 1
Relative	5	< 1	10
Mother	41	< 1	49
Father	1	0	< 1
Sibling	4	2	3
Self-care	3	2	5
Non-relative	1	6	8
Other or missing	12	10	5
Number of observations	53	161	198

[a] *School-age care* is before- and after-school care provided for children age 6–12.

civilian programs appearing to be more popular than DoD programs. Hours of operation and reliability of the care rank as the most important reasons for selecting civilian after-school care.

Dual-Military Families

As shown in Table 4.1, the majority of dual-military families with children age 0–5 use child-care centers. DoD CDC care was most commonly reported (42 percent), while 13 percent use civilian child-care centers, and 12 percent use civilian family child care.

The popularity of CDC care is, again, not surprising, given the preference offered to dual-military families. Just under half of dual-military parents using a CDC cited the level of quality as the most important reason for selecting this care, with cost as the second most-important consideration. The relative position of cost is not surprising, since cost of CDC care based on total family income is substantially higher for dual-income families than it is for single parents. It is somewhat surprising that dual-military families are not using FCC to a greater extent, because these families likely need flexible, extended hours of care. In addition, it is probable that the cost of FCC is comparable to that of the CDC for dual-military families, because the higher dual-family income would likely put most of these families into a high CDC fee category. However, other factors may explain the low usage of FCC by dual-military parents, according to some participants in the RAND focus groups conducted for this study. Parents told us that, on some installations, FCC providers choose to limit their hours of operation and provide no holiday care.[2] In theory, FCC providers can provide flexible, extended hours of care, but unless they are receiving a direct subsidy, they are not obliged to do so.[3]

---

[2] For example, some FCC providers serve only the children of teachers so that they need to work only during the school year and are off in the summer and on school vacations. Focus group wives told us that some FCC providers require that children leave the FCC site before the time that their husbands come home, which limits the flexibility and availability of FCC care in such situations.

[3] Some, but not all, locations that offer subsidies require that those who receive them comply with Major Command or Service policies concerning hours of operation.

The majority of dual-military families with children age 6–12 (61 percent) reported using a civilian after-school program as the primary care arrangement. Some dual-military families choose DoD after-school programs, but to a much lesser extent (13 percent). Three percent use civilian FCC, while less than 1 percent use DoD FCC. The preference for civilian after-school programs was reportedly due to their hours of operation and location, both of which were factors cited by parents who were surveyed. Focus group participants in some locations told us that there was no transportation from the local elementary school to the DoD after-school program on base, which meant that the on-base program was not an option. Ninety-seven percent of families using civilian family child care for this age group cited hours of operation as the most important factor leading them to choose this type of care.

Military-Member-Married-to-Civilian Families

By far the most common form of child-care arrangement for families of military members married to civilians with children age 0–5 is care by the children's mother (41 percent), as shown in Table 4.1. Lower percentages of families in this group use the DoD CDC (11 percent), DoD FCC (11 percent), or civilian child-care centers (12 percent).

Sixty-seven percent of these families in which the mother is the primary caregiver reported that the civilian spouse is not working outside the home. In a survey of military spouses regarding employment issues, Harrell et al. (2004) found that a majority of civilian spouses of military members were not employed nor seeking full-time employment due to parenting responsibilities. A sizable number of these parents cited child-care problems as a barrier to employment. Other barriers included the demands of the military lifestyle and limited employment options in the local area. In our survey, we asked what the most important reasons were for choosing maternal care; 24 percent of parents cited cost as the key reason, and 36 percent cited wanting a family environment for their children.

Care provided by the mother of a child is also the most frequent form of care among families with a military member and civilian spouse with children age 6–12; it accounted for more than all other types of care combined (49 percent). Civilian after-school programs are used by some of these families (5 percent), as are the DoD SAC (1 percent) and DoD youth center (4 percent). Almost one-third (30 percent) of those families using the mother as the primary caregiver reported cost as the most important reason for choosing that type of care.

Child-Care Choice

In our analysis of child-care choice, we examined whether a family uses parental care or not, and, then, for those families who do not use parental care, we explored the question of which child-care option they choose. We then asked parents why they chose a particular option. Not surprisingly, the factors that influence the decision to use parental care differ from the factors influencing the type of non-parental care used, and the factors differ by the child's age.

Table 4.3 summarizes the statistically significant relationships among the child-care variables and the probability that a family uses parental care. In each case, the differences are measured in relation to the omitted category in the regression model used in this analysis. The results are summarized for preschool-age and school-age children.[4] For a categorical variable, such as family type, a plus sign indicates that the designated category or group is more likely than the omitted category to use parental care, while a minus sign indicates that the designated category or group is less likely to use parental care. For example, Table 4.3 suggests that, among families with preschool-age children, families with a working or non-working civilian spouse are more likely than single military parents to use parental care. For a continuous variable, such as local median income, the plus sign reflects that, as that variable increases, the probability of using parental care increases. Conversely, a minus sign reflects that, as the variable increases, the probability of using parental care decreases. Thus, Table 4.3 suggests that, among families with school-age children, those families who live in areas with higher local median incomes are more likely to use parental care.

---

[4] For more details on the analytic results, see Gates et al. (2006).

Table 4.3
Factors Related to the Probability of Families Using Parental Care for Preschool-Age and School-Age Children

Variable	Preschool-Age Children	School-Age Children
Family Type		
Dual military	N/A	–
Working civilian spouse	+	N/A
Non-working civilian spouse	+	+
Single military parent		
Family Income		
< $25,000	N/A	N/A
< $50,000	N/A	+
$75,000 +		
Distance between home and base		
Live on base		
Ten miles or less	+	N/A
Rank		
Officer	N/A	–
Enlisted		
Local median income	N/A	+
Local child-care supply	–	+

NOTES: For type of child care, DoD CDC is the omitted category for preschool-age children, and civilian formal care (care that includes both civilian CDC and FCC care) is the omitted category for school-age children.

NA = not applicable or not statistically significant. Grayed-out cells indicate omitted category in the regression model.

Decision to Use Parental Child Care

Compared with single military parents, civilian families with working and non-working spouses are more likely to use parental care for their preschool-age children. Families who live off base, but within ten miles of the installation, are more likely than those on base to use parental care for preschool-age children. Families who live in a community with a greater supply of child-care workers are less likely to use parental care for their preschool-age children. It is evident that in areas where the supply of non-DoD child-care options is greater, civilian spouses are more likely to work outside the home and use that care.

We found similar results for families with school-age children. In addition, families with children age 6–12 and with incomes less than $50,000 per year are more likely to use parental care than families whose income is above $75,000. Dual-military families are less likely than single-parent families to use parental care. Families whose highest-ranking military member is an officer are more likely than families of enlisted personnel to use parental care for their school-age children. Finally, families living in areas with higher median incomes are more likely to use parental care for their school-age children.

Decision to Use Non-Parental Child Care

Tables 4.4 and 4.5 summarize the statistically significant relationships among independent variables and the probability that a family uses a particular type of non-parental care. The tables are interpreted in the same way as Table 4.3.

Family income plays a significant role in the particular child-care options that families choose once they decide to rely on non-parental care. Families earning less than $75,000 per year are less likely to use FCC than the CDC compared with families earning more than $75,000 per year. This may be due to the fact that families who receive larger subsidies (and hence pay less) for CDC care are more likely to use that care. We also find that families in which the work hours of the parents vary are less likely to use FCC relative to the CDC.

Proximity to an installation is also an important factor in child-care choice. Families living between 11 and 20 miles from an installation are less likely to use FCC than CDC care compared with families that live on base. Across the board, families living off base are more likely to choose formal civilian child-care options over the DoD CDC, and propensity to use civilian child care increases as the distance from an installation grows. Many of our focus group participants reported that they prefer the convenience of having their child-care arrangement near their home; this is found to be true in research studies of the civilian population as well (e.g., Queralt and Witte, 1999). Families who live off base but near the installation are more likely to use care options other than the CDC. This may be because those living off an installation have a wider array of choices available to them, and their

Table 4.4
Factors Related to the Probability of Families Using Various Child-Care Options, Families Using Non-Parental Care for Preschool-Age Children

Variable Name	DoD CDC	DoD FCC	Civilian Formal Care	Other Care
Family type				
Dual military	N/A	N/A	–	N/A
Single military parent				
Work hours vary week to week				
Yes	N/A	–	N/A	–
No				
Family income				
< $25,000	N/A	–	N/A	N/A
$25,000–$49,999	N/A	–	N/A	N/A
$50,000–$74,999	N/A	–	N/A	N/A
$75,000 +				
Distance between home and base				
Live on base				
Ten miles or less	N/A	N/A	+	N/A
11–20 miles	N/A	N/A	+	N/A
More than 20 miles	N/A	N/A	+	–
Rank				
Officer	N/A	–	N/A	N/A
Enlisted				
Reservist				
Yes	N/A	+	N/A	+
No				
Service				
Air Force				
Marines	N/A	–	–	N/A
Local female unemployment rate	N/A	–	N/A	N/A
Local median income	N/A	N/A	–	–
Local child-care supply	N/A	N/A	N/A	+

NOTES: For type of child care, DoD CDC is the omitted category for preschool-age children.

NA = not applicable or not statistically significant. Grayed-out cells indicate omitted category in the regression model.

Table 4.5
Factors Related to the Probability of Families Using Various Child-Care Options, Families Using Non-Parental Care for School-Age Children

Variable	All DoD Care	Civilian Formal Care	Other Care
Family type			
Non-working civilian spouse	N/A	–	+
Single military parent			
Work hours vary week to week			
Yes	N/A	–	–
No			
Family income			
< $50,000	N/A	–	+
$50,000–$74,999	N/A	–	–
$75,000 +			
Distance between home and base			
Live on base			
Ten miles or less	N/A	+	+
11–20 miles	N/A	+	+
More than 20 miles	N/A	+	+
Reservist			
Yes	N/A	–	+
No			
Family has another child age 13–18			
Yes	N/A	N/A	+
No			

NOTES: For type of child care, DoD CDC is the omitted category for preschool-age children, and civilian formal care is the omitted category for school-age children. NA = not applicable or not statistically significant. Grayed-out cells indicate omitted category in the regression model.

preference may be for other kinds of care. This suggests that proximity to home is an important consideration for families in their child-care choice; families who live off base (and particularly those who live far from the installation) are less likely to use DoD-sponsored care options, which overwhelmingly are located on base.

Relative to the Air Force, survey respondents in the Marine Corps were more likely to choose CDC care over FCC or formal civilian care options. Reservists were more likely to use FCC and other care options than the CDC. This preference may be due to the short window of time that reserve families have to secure child care when they are called up; CDCs often have long waiting lists and cannot accommodate these families on short notice. In addition, many reserve families may not live near an installation, so accessing a DoD CDC is not an option for them. FCC and other child-care options may be the only options available for reserve families and may provide more flexibility than the DoD CDC. Families living in areas with higher median incomes are less likely to use formal civilian care options, while families living in areas with a large supply of child-care workers are more likely to use civilian formal care options and other informal care options as opposed to the CDC. If we assume that the cost of civilian child care is higher in areas where median incomes are higher, it would suggest that military families are willing to use civilian child-care options when those options are available and affordable.

The results from the analysis of families with school-age children (see Table 4.5) reveal a relationship between various family and installation characteristics and child-care choice. Families who have a child between the ages of 13 and 18 in addition to a preschooler or elementary-school-age child are much more likely to use other informal care options than those who do not. Most likely, the teenage children care for the younger ones. Families with a civilian spouse who does not work outside the home but who use some form of non-parental care are much less likely to use DoD-sponsored forms of care for their school-age children than single military parents. This is no doubt because DoD-sponsored care is geared for working spouses and, indeed, one must be working to access CDCs. Across the board, families living off base are more likely to use formal civilian child-care options and other informal options than DoD-sponsored child-care options. Families who live in areas where the female unemployment rate is high are more likely to use other, informal types of child care. Families of officers are more likely to use formal civilian care options and informal care options, relative to families of enlisted members.

Family type, income, and service influence the likelihood of using parental care. Once a decision is made to use non-parental care, family income and proximity to an installation are the major determinants of the type of care that is used.

Use of Multiple Arrangements

One way of determining whether existing child-care options are meeting the needs of military families is to consider whether families are relying on multiple care arrangements to ensure an adequate amount of care for their children. We asked military parents to report whether they used an additional arrangement in the past week, and, if so, the reasons for using that care. In this section, we look at the use of multiple child-care arrangements by family type and by type of care, to better understand the characteristics of families that are using multiple arrangements and how multiple care arrangements are constructed.

Tables 4.6 and 4.7 show the use of multiple child-care arrangements, by family type, according to the type of primary care used by families with children age 0–5 and children age 6–12, respectively. Tables 4.8 and 4.9 show the number of hours that a secondary child-care arrangement was used by families according to the type of primary arrangement used by families with children age 0–5 and children age 6–12, respectively.

All Family Types

Twenty-one percent of all families reported using more than one child-care arrangement in the past week; very few families reported using more than one additional arrangement. Among families who reported using one or more additional arrangements in the past week, the vast majority used additional arrangements for ten or fewer hours per week. These other arrangements tend to be informal ones: relatives or non-relatives in-home or outside the home.

Table 4.6
Percentage of Families with Children Age 0–5 Using Multiple Child-Care Arrangements, by Family Type

Primary Arrangement	Single Parent	Dual Military	Civilian Spouse
DoD CDC	33	14	15
DoD FCC	0	95	14
DoD SAC	N/A	53	N/A
Civilian after-school program	0	54	100
Civilian child-care center	13	2	9
Civilian FCC	41	90	93
Relative	30	98	0
Mother	4	0	25
Father	N/A	0	0
Sibling	N/A	0	0
Self-care	0	0	0
Non-relative	63	97	15
Other or missing	19	92	46
Overall percentage using more than one child-care arrangement	21	48	27
Number of observations	58	241	162

NOTE: N/A = not applicable or not statistically significant.

Single Parents

Twenty-one percent of single parents with children age 0–5 reported that they used at least one other child-care arrangement in addition to their primary arrangement in the past week (see Table 4.6). A large fraction of families using the DoD CDC used secondary arrangements, as did those using civilian centers. Indeed, our focus group participants using the CDC cited the need to use multiple arrangements to work around the limited hours of the CDC and the rule on some bases limiting the time that children may be in care to a maximum of ten hours per day. In sharp contrast to these findings, none of the single-parent families who reported using a DoD FCC said that they had to use a secondary child-care arrangement in the past week. However, 41 percent of single parents using a civilian FCC said that they used more than one

Table 4.7
Percentage of Families with Children Age 6–12 Using Multiple Child-Care Arrangements, by Family Type

Primary Arrangement	Single Parent	Dual Military	Civilian Spouse
DoD CDC	0	0	10
DoD FCC	N/A	20	0
DoD SAC	12	3	0
DoD youth center	14	18	27
DoD after-school program	74	< 1	0
Civilian after-school program	10	33	6
Civilian child-care center	72	32	10
Civilian FCC	57	1	0
Relative	53	0	20
Mother	1	< 1	17
Father	0	N/A	0
Sibling	0	0	0
Self-care	52	89	0
Non-relative	0	35	26
Other or missing	0	0	64
Overall percentage using more than one child-care arrangement	11	23	16
Number of observations	56	164	201

NOTE: N/A = not applicable or not statistically significant.

arrangement. A large percentage of single-parent families using informal care provided by relatives and non-relatives inside and outside the home reported using more than one arrangement in the past week.

As shown in Table 4.8, families with children age 0–5 who use the DoD CDC are using, on average, seven hours of additional care per week. A large fraction of those parents (53 percent) reported that they needed additional care in the past week due to work hours that extended beyond the child-care center hours.

Despite being open long hours—typical hours of operation are 6 a.m. to 6 p.m. in the case of the CDCs—this period of time does

Table 4.8
Number of Hours the Secondary Child-Care Arrangement Was Used in the Past Week, by Primary Arrangement and Family Type, Families with Children Age 0–5

Primary Arrangement	Single Parent	Dual Military	Military Married to Civilian
DoD CDC	7	8	36
DoD FCC	0	9 [a]	3
Civilian formal care	18	5	8
Overall	14	8	14

[a] These estimates are based on very few observations; the estimate for 0- to 5-year-olds is based on five observations.

Table 4.9
Number of Hours the Secondary Child-Care Arrangement Was Used in the Past Week, by Primary Arrangement and Family Type, by Families with Children Age 6–12

Primary Arrangement	Single Parent	Dual Military	Military Married to Civilian
DoD CDC	8	10	5
DoD FCC	0	20 [a]	0
Civilian formal care	21	5	13
Overall	18	5	6

[a] These estimates are based on very few observations; the estimate for 6- to 12-year-olds is based on one observation.

not completely cover duty hours for some parents.[5] In our focus groups with military parents, single parents in particular described the difficulty of managing child care given the CDC's limited hours. Some must leave work early to pick up their children from the CDC and take them to another care provider before returning to work. Others make arrangements with care providers or friends to pick up their children from their primary provider and care for them until they are off duty. One focus group participant described being part of a cooperative child-care arrangement that included a group of single parents working

[5] The DoD has experimented with extended CDC hours but found that the small number of parents using those hours did not justify the high fixed costs.

together in a unit in shifts from 8 a.m. to 8 p.m. Parents also organize their schedules so that they are off duty on staggered days. On off days, they provide supplemental care for the other parents still on duty after regular child care closes.

Our data indicate that military FCC, which typically provides parents with the flexibility to use extended hours of care after regular work hours and on weekends, is successful in reducing use of multiple arrangements, at least for single parents. Families using civilian FCC seemingly have less flexibility in the hours of care provided, as evidenced by the high percentage of families of each type using this care that reported using an additional arrangement. A high percentage of those families using informal care arrangements reported needing additional care to cover shift work, weekend work, and extended hours. Some also reported unexpected child-care needs that required them to use supplemental care. A vast majority of these families are using a patchwork of options to cover their child-care needs. Stitching together this care is difficult, stressful, and time-consuming, although having multiple providers may afford some measure of security in the event that one provider is unavailable.

Overall, the use of secondary care arrangements by single-parent families with children age 6–12 does not appear to be extensive: 11 percent of these families reported using supplemental care in the past week (see Table 4.7). Care provided by the mother is the largest source of primary care among this group (41 percent), and only 1 percent of these families report using additional care arrangements. Those primarily using care provided by a relative report the highest prevalence of secondary care arrangements (53 percent), but these families represent a very small proportion (2 percent) of all single-parent families with children age 6–12.

Dual-Military Families

The use of supplemental care is much more prevalent among dual-military families with children age 0–5 than among other family types; 48 percent of dual-military families reported using at least one secondary arrangement (see Table 4.6). The use of additional arrangements is particularly high among dual-military families using FCC, which is somewhat surprising, since, in theory, FCC can provide more-flexible arrangements to support extended hours or irregular schedules relative to other formal care arrangements, and it appears to do so for single-parent families. Nearly 90 percent of families using civilian FCC and 95 percent of those using DoD FCC used at least one other child-care arrangement in the past week.

On average, dual-military families used 8.4 hours of care to supplement their regular arrangement. Twenty-six percent of these families reported unexpected child-care need as a reason for using supplemental care. One explanation for the high percentage of families with supplemental arrangements could be that some FCC providers' hours do not cover duty times: Closures for training days, holidays, or personal vacations may force parents into finding supplemental care. In our focus groups with military parents, many parents cited this aspect of FCC as a major challenge they encountered in using FCC. Although some DoD FCC providers are required to have a back-up provider, this is not a uniform requirement at all installations, and even when it is required, parents reported that the policy does not work in practice because back-up providers do not keep spaces open on a consistent basis.

Among dual-military families with children age 6–12, 23 percent use one or more secondary arrangements to supplement their primary child care (see Table 4.7). In sharp contrast to the dual-military families using civilian FCC in the 0–5-years age group, a very low percentage of dual-military families in the 6–12-years age group (1 percent) reported using any additional care in the past week. A majority of families in this category use civilian after-school care as the primary care arrangement, and roughly 33 percent of them report an additional care arrangement. These families supplement their care with about five hours in an additional child-care arrangement (see Table 4.9). Ninety-nine percent of these families reported that they need the supplemental care to cover extended hours at work.

Military-Married-to-Civilian Families

Among families with a civilian spouse and with children age 0–5, 27 percent are using secondary child-care arrangements (see Table 4.6). Most notably, 25 percent of families in which the mother is the primary caregiver use another arrangement. Families using the DoD CDC and DoD FCC as their primary care arrangement appear to use secondary arrangements to some extent (15 percent and 14 percent, respectively).

Military-married-to-civilian families with children age 0–5 reported using an average of 14 hours of care to supplement their primary care arrangement (see Table 4.8). DoD CDC users reported the largest number of hours of secondary-arrangement use (36 hours), while DoD FCC users reported three hours of use.

Fifty-five percent of military-married-to-civilian families with children age 0–5 in which the mother is the primary caregiver reported unexpected child-care need as a reason for using additional care; 19 percent reported that additional care was needed because a parent was in school. These parents reported using this care for 11 hours in the past week on average.

Military-married-to-civilian families with children age 6–12 use a supplementary care arrangement to a lesser extent than do those with children age 0–5. While most school-age children in families with a civilian spouse are cared for primarily by their mothers, 17 percent of these families use supplemental care. Users of DoD CDC and civilian child-care center care used the most hours of additional care. One-hundred percent of these families cited working extended hours as the reason for using additional care arrangements.

Unmet Need

As noted in Chapter One, our study employs a fairly broad definition of *unmet need*: situations in which parents report that they would like to use a formal child-care arrangement but are not doing so. Families with unmet need include those who use any informal care arrangement (such as a relative or a non-relative in or outside the home) or parental, sibling, or self-care *and* report that they would prefer another option. This definition does not include families who are currently using some sort of formal child-care arrangement, even if they report that it is not their preferred option. Similarly, the definition of unmet need does not include families who are using an informal arrangement or parental care unless they also report that they would prefer some other option.

Our survey found that nearly 9 percent of parents have unmet need. The analysis reveals that families are more likely to report unmet need for children between the age of 0 and 5 than for older children. Dual-military families are less likely than single-parent families to report unmet need, whereas military members with civilian working spouses are more likely than single parents to report unmet need. This finding may be due to the preference given to single-parent and dual-military families in the DoD system, specifically in the CDCs, and it suggests that the DoD policy has been generally successful in meeting the child-care needs of these families.

The analysis also indicates that the income level of a military family is related to unmet need among parents of preschool-age children. Compared with families that had earnings greater than $75,000 in 2003, families earning less than that amount were more likely to report unmet need. Families earning less than $25,000 per year were four percentage points more likely to report unmet need, and families earning between $25,000 and $50,000 per year were 18 percentage points more likely to report unmet need. Families earning between $50,000 and $75,000 were two percentage points more likely to report unmet need. One can speculate that families on the low end of the income distribution are more likely to express unmet need because the lack of child care prevents a civilian spouse from working outside the home, thus contributing to low family income.

Among families of children between the ages of 6 and 12, we find no statistically significant relationship between family or installation characteristics and reports of unmet need. This finding may be due to the fact that so few families with children in this age range report any unmet need.

Unmet Preference

We also examined *unmet preference*, i.e., parents who report that their current child-care arrangement is not their first choice, regardless of what type of care they are using. While relatively few families report unmet child-care need, we found that many more parents report unmet preference. Overall, 22 percent of survey respondents indicated that they would prefer another child-care arrangement to the one they are currently using. Parents of preschool-age children are more likely to report unmet preference than are parents of school-age children.

Table 4.10 summarizes the child-care preferences of families who responded to the survey with a preference for another care arrangement.

The results of the analysis reveal that there is considerable unmet preference for DoD formal child care among military families. If we group together families expressing a preference for DoD CDC or DoD school-age care, youth center programs, and after-school programs, the

Table 4.10
Type of Care Preferred by Parents Who Expressed Unmet Preference

Primary Arrangement	Percentage of Parents with Children Age 0–5	Percentage of Parents with Children Age 6–12
DoD CDC	56	4
DoD FCC	6	1
DoD SAC	1	3
DoD youth center	< 1	8
DoD after-school program	2	19
Civilian after-school program	< 1	24
Civilian child-care center	10	< 1
Civilian FCC	< 1	< 1
Relative	15	20
Mother	2	8
Father	< 1	< 1
Self-care	0	< 1
Non-relative	9	13
Other or missing	< 1	0
Number of observations	147	74

total percentage of parents with unmet preference for structured DoD programs would be 49 percent.[6]

While many parents expressed a preference for DoD-sponsored care, it is also the case that many families who currently use DoD-sponsored care stated a preference for some other form of care.[7] Nearly one-third of DoD FCC users, DoD CDC users, and those using formal civilian care options say they would prefer another option, including another DoD option. Only about one-third of the families who report unmet preference report that a DoD-sponsored arrangement is their first choice.

Among parents of children age 0–5, those whose work hours vary are more than twice as likely to report unmet preference. This suggests that many child-care arrangements may not match well with irregular military schedules. More than half of families responding to the survey with children age 0–5 reported that the work hours of at least one parent varied from week to week. This is true for a large percentage of single-parent and dual-military families. In addition, as discussed above, use of multiple arrangements is quite extensive among our survey respondents. The need for multiple arrangements may underlie dissatisfaction with current arrangements and contribute to unmet preference.

In examining the differences among services, we found that unmet preference is highest for the Air Force. Relative to Air Force families, Army and Marine Corps[8] families are less likely (by 21 percentage points and 39 percentage points, respectively) to report unmet

---

[6] The high level of unmet preference for CDC care is consistent with findings from the April 2004 Status on Forces Survey (Defense Manpower Data Center, 2004), which found that CDC care was preferred by a higher percentage of respondents (26 percent) than any other care option.

[7] It is worth emphasizing here and in other discussions of the differences among families using different types of child care that families using one type of child care may differ in observed and unobserved ways from families using other types of care. These differences may be related to the outcome under consideration.

[8] In this regression analysis, there were not enough observations from the Marine Corps to analyze those observations separately, so they were combined with the Navy observations.

child-care preference for preschool-age children, holding all other factors constant.

Among parents of school-age children, we found that those using civilian-run formal child-care arrangements were more likely than those using DoD-sponsored arrangements or parental care to report unmet preference. Dual-military families were 61 percentage points more likely than single parents to report unmet preference, while families who have variable work hours were more likely than families with regular work hours to report unmet preference.

Families using civilian formal child-care arrangements were substantially more likely (more than twice as likely) than families using other types of care to report unmet preference. The relatively high level of unmet preference among those using civilian child-care arrangements may be due to a lack of DoD-sponsored child care for school-age children or to logistical barriers that render DoD-sponsored options inconvenient for many families. Indeed, as discussed above, some focus group participants said that they could not use DoD-sponsored school-age care because there was no way to get their children from school to the DoD program.

Child Care and Military Readiness

To assess the impact of child-care issues on military readiness, the survey asked whether child-care issues kept parents from reporting for military duty, caused military members to be late for work or to miss work, or had an effect on deployments.

Reporting for Duty

To some extent, child-care issues appear to influence the ability of military members to report for duty (see Table 4.11). A considerable fraction of single-parent families and dual-military families with children age 0–5 reported that lack of child care after the birth of a child or after first moving to their current installation kept them from reporting for military duty (11 percent and 36 percent, respectively). On average, single parents of children age 0–5 reported that it took them

Table 4.11
Families with Children Age 0–5 Responding that Lack of Child Care Prevented a Parent from Reporting for Military Duty

Family Type	Percentage of Families
Single parent	11
Dual military	36
Military member married to civilian spouse	< 1

3.1 months to find care after the birth of the target child; dual-military families reported an average of 1.8 months of search time; the search time for families with a civilian spouse was 2.2 months.

Late to Work or Missed Work

In the analyses on readiness, we wanted to focus on military parents. Consequently, we include in these analyses any family type that includes a military mother or father. These parents could live in single-parent, dual-military, or married-to-civilian families.

The impact of child-care issues on military readiness appears to be greater for female than for male military members. Among all families with a military mother, 51 percent reported that the military mother was late to work due to child-care issues in the past month. For families with a military father, 22 percent of survey respondents reported that the military father was late to work due to child-care issues in the past month. This tended to happen one or two times in the past month, but for some, it happened up to 20 times. Similarly, among families with a military father, 7 percent reported that the military father missed work due to child-care issues in the past month. For families with a military mother, the figure was 37 percent for mothers missing work. Clearly, military women are carrying a bigger load in terms of child care; they cover for child-care inadequacies to a greater degree than do male military members.

Deployments

Deployments appear to have some impact on the child-care arrangements of military families, but finding care after deployment is not reported to be a major challenge for most military families. Not surprisingly, more single-parent and dual-military families with children age 0–5 reported that their child-care arrangements changed as a result of their most recent deployment than did military members married to civilians (see Table 4.12). The most common changes among these families were to withdraw from the DoD child-care system, arrange for more care, or move the child elsewhere during the deployment. Single parents with preschool-age children reported the most difficulty in getting the child care they needed after the deployment was over: 67 percent of those parents said finding care post-deployment was difficult or very difficult. The majority of dual-military parents and military members married to a civilian reported that finding care was not at all difficult post-deployment (58 percent and 57 percent, respectively). Among families with school-age children, more dual-military families (32 percent) than single parents or military members married to civilian families reported a change in their child-care arrangements. Approximately 8 percent of both single-parent families and families with a civilian spouse said that arranging care after deployment was difficult. Fifty-nine percent of dual-military families reported that it was somewhat difficult to find care post-deployment.

Likelihood of Leaving the Military

Given that few families reported unmet child-care need, it is noteworthy that 21 percent of families responding to our survey reported that it was likely or very likely that they would leave the military because of

Table 4.12
Families Reporting that Child Care Changed Due to Deployment

Family Type	Percentage of Families with Children Age 0–5	Percentage of Families with Children Age 6–12
Single parent	21	24
Dual military	23	32
Military member married to civilian	12	9

child-care issues. These findings suggest that unmet need alone is an insufficient indicator of the toll that finding and using child care and raising young children in a military setting takes on families.

Families with children age 0–5 were much more likely than families with school-age children to report a propensity to leave the military. This difference may be partially due to the fact that the parents of older children tend to be older themselves, and have a longer tenure in and stronger commitment to a military career. Our analyses suggest that family status and service-related differences appear to have a strong relationship to plans to leave the service.

Among families with children age 0–5, dual-military parents were substantially more likely (by 30 percentage points) than single parents to consider leaving the military due to child-care concerns, whereas the probability for families with civilian working or non-working spouses was lower (but not statistically significantly different from the probability for single parents). This suggests that, despite policies that favor single-parent and dual-military families in terms of CDC enrollment, parents in these families still find it difficult to balance military work and family demands.

The type of child-care arrangement currently used also relates to reports of propensity to leave the service. Compared with parents in families using DoD CDCs, parents in families using all other care arrangements, including DoD FCC, for their preschool-age children are substantially less likely to report that they are considering leaving the military due to child-care issues. The results show that families of military officers are less likely to report that a parent has considered leaving the military due to child-care issues than families of enlisted personnel.

We found similar results for families with children age 6–12. As with younger children, the findings suggest that, despite policies that favor single-parent and dual-military families in terms of program enrollment, these parents still find it difficult to balance military work and family demands. Those whose work hours vary from week to week and reservists are more likely to report having considered leaving the service because of child-care issues.

For military members married to civilians, spousal employment issues may be a factor in influencing a military member's propensity to remain in the military. If the spouse would like to work, but a lack of child-care options prevents him or her from finding a job, this might ultimately influence the military member's decision to remain in the military. The survey asked respondents whether child-care issues affected a civilian spouse's ability to find employment. Nineteen percent of families with a military member married to a civilian spouse with children age 0–5 reported that lack of child care kept the civilian spouse from looking for work, and 18 percent reported that it kept the civilian spouse from beginning his or her civilian job. Parents of school-age children reported much less impact on employment than families with preschool-age children, with the exception of military-member-married-to-civilian families. Twenty-three percent of those families indicated that lack of child care inhibited a parent's ability to look for civilian work; smaller percentages of those parents reported that it impacted their ability to start a civilian job or kept them from attending school.

Summary

Although previous research has suggested that child-care issues are a concern for many military families with a civilian spouse, our survey results provide a more nuanced and complete understanding of the child-care challenges facing all military families and the potential implications for the DoD.

Although Rare, Unmet Need for Child Care Is an Issue for Certain Military Families

Although relatively few families experience unmet need, our results show that families with preschool-age children, families with a military member married to a civilian, and those in the lowest income brackets are more likely to experience unmet need than other families. This suggests that it is important to continue to focus resources on providing care for preschool-age children. Policies designed to give preference to single-parent and dual-military families for DoD care appear to be effective in reducing unmet need among these families. However, among families with a civilian spouse, a lack of child care may prevent the civilian spouse from working outside the home, with implications for family income and the spouse's satisfaction.

Unmet Preference Is More Common than Unmet Need

A higher percentage of families experience unmet preference than unmet need. Unmet preference is greater among families with preschool-age children and those whose work hours vary. There is unmet preference for formal DoD child care, but there is also unmet preference among those using formal DoD child care for other types of care. Forty-four percent of families who report unmet preference express a preference for DoD care. That means that more than half of the families expressing unmet preference would like something other than what the DoD currently provides.

Child-Care Issues Impact the Readiness of Military Members

We found that child-care issues impact the readiness of military members, and some are impacted more than others. Single-parent and dual-military families with children age 0–5 reported challenges in finding child care after the birth of the target child or when they moved to an installation, which prevented them from reporting for military duty. Single parents in particular reported long search times for child-care arrangements.

The readiness impact of child-care issues appears to be greater for female than male military members; mothers more often than fathers are covering for child-care inadequacies by being late for work or missing work entirely.

While deployments have some effect on child-care arrangements, finding care following the end of deployment is generally described as not being a significant problem for most military families. A key exception to that generalization is single parents, who report that they experience difficulty reentering the child-care system after a deployment is over.

Single and Dual-Military Parents Favor CDCs but Use Multiple Arrangements to Satisfy Child-Care Need

It appears that CDCs and civilian centers are the most popular forms of care among single-parent and dual-military families. A large fraction of single-parent and dual-military families are using center-based care for their children age 0–5. Many of these parents are using the DoD CDC, and they cite cost, availability, and quality as the most important reasons for choosing the CDC. It appears that the enrollment preference for both groups and the large subsidy for single-parent families (because fees are based on total family income) may be influencing their use of this care. A larger percentage of single-parent families reports using civilian centers than DoD CDCs and reports that hours of operation and cost are the most important reasons for selecting this type of care. This suggests that civilian centers (at least in some low-cost locations) may be less expensive and more convenient than other options for these families.

Many parents using CDCs also use an additional child-care provider. These parents typically report that they are using multiple child-care arrangements because their work hours extend past CDC hours of operation. Single-parent and dual-military families are not using FCC on a widespread basis. This is somewhat surprising since, in theory, FCC can provide parents with the flexible, extended hours of care that single-parent and dual-military families typically need. However, the cost, hours of operation, and other factors (e.g., safety concerns) make FCC less attractive to these families. Preference for spaces given to single-parent and dual-military families in DoD CDCs may also make FCC care a less attractive choice for many parents. Our focus group participants suggested, however, that the longer and more flexible hours FCC can provide are not always provided in practice. In fact, some providers choose to severely limit their hours, not offering even full-time care, let alone after-hours care and weekend care. These focus group parents told us that the most important reasons for their not using FCC care are the inconvenience and unreliability associated with dependence on a single individual that characterizes this form of care.

Local Market Conditions Are Related to the Child-Care Choices that DoD Families Make

Although DoD-sponsored care is an important child-care option for military families, it is not the only option. Our analysis reveals that families with preschool-age children who live in areas with lower median incomes and families who live in areas with a greater supply of child-care workers are more likely to use civilian child care than DoD-sponsored care.

Although Formal Civilian Child-Care Options Are Used Widely for School-Age Children, They May Not Be Preferred

Formal civilian after-school programs and child-care centers, and, to a lesser extent, civilian family child care, are widely used by all family types for children age 6–12. Many of these parents cite hours of operation, location, reliability, and cost as the major reasons for using civilian care. Interestingly, these families who use civilian formal child care are more likely to experience unmet preference than those using DoD-sponsored child care for school-age children. This higher rate of unmet preference among users of civilian care may reflect a lack of DoD school-age care, inconvenient locations, or inconvenient hours for DoD care. Focus group participants told us that DoD school-age care often did not coordinate well with local schools, making use of such care impossible. On one installation, for example, there was no transportation from the local, off-base elementary school to the after-school program on base.

Families Living Off Base Are Less Likely to Use DoD-Sponsored Care

The distance between a family's home and an installation is strongly related to the type of child care the family uses. Families who live off base are less likely to use DoD-sponsored child-care options, and the propensity to use DoD-sponsored care is lower the farther families live from base. These families do seem to find other options that meet their needs, given that they are not more likely to express unmet need.

DoD CDC Users Appear to Have a Weaker Attachment to the Military

Our analysis reveals that, controlling for family type, families who use the DoD CDCs are more likely than families who use other care options to report that they are likely to leave the military due to child-care issues.

CHAPTER FIVE

Conclusions and Recommendations

In this monograph, we use the results of a nationwide survey of military families and a small number of focus groups to assess DoD's child-care demand formula. We discuss the difference between potential need, as calculated by the demand formula, and the actual need for DoD-sponsored child-care space. We also assess the ability of the formula to accurately project potential child-care need. In addressing the latter issue, we compare the assumptions of the DoD formula with the survey data. We also discuss the implications of the survey results for DoD child-care policy.

Conclusions

Some aspects of DoD's child-care demand formula deserve attention. Two in particular stand out. First, the formula relies on DEERS data for its demographic estimates. We found differences, some of them substantial, between family status reported in DEERS and family status reported by survey respondents. Because the formula makes fundamentally different assumptions about the potential need for child care among families of different types, it is important for the DoD to have an accurate estimate of the family status of military members who have minor dependents.

There are several potential explanations for the differences we observed in family status distributions between DEERS data and our survey responses. One likely explanation is that family status is dynamic. We sampled families using DEERS data from September

2003, but we did not mail the surveys until early 2004. During this time, we would expect some couples to marry and others to divorce, leading some military members to accurately report a different family type than what appears in the DEERS data. It is, however, unlikely that the substantial differences observed would be completely explained by marriage and divorce over a three- to nine-month period. Another explanation is that the quality of the marital status information in the DEERS file is low. A primary purpose of the DEERS is to maintain information on benefits eligibility. Therefore, military members have a strong incentive to update their marital status when they marry (if they are marrying someone who does not already qualify for benefits), but not when they divorce. Nor could we rely on a dual-military flag in the DEERS data to help us identify dual-military families, because DEERS no longer includes a flag denoting families of that type. This poses substantial challenges for DoD in identifying those families.

It is certainly plausible that some of the divergence between the DEERS data and our survey data can be accounted for by the low response rate of our survey. To account for non-response bias, however, we used weighted data in reporting and analyzing the results of the survey.

The survey results also raise questions about some of the DoD child-care demand formula's basic assumptions regarding the use of child care among different types of families. The formula takes into account the fact that DoD-sponsored child care is needed only when the child lives with a military member and makes assumptions about the proportion of children who live with their military parent. For families with a civilian spouse, the formula also makes assumptions about the proportion of civilian spouses who work outside the home or attend school and the proportion of those civilian spouses who are working full time. Children with a non-working civilian parent are not included in the calculation of potential child-care need.

When we compared our survey data with the formula's assumptions regarding the fraction of children who live with their parents and spousal employment rates, we found substantial differences between the two sets of data. Although the use of weighted data, discussed above, increases the standard error of our point estimates, we still find statistically significant differences between the formula parameters and the survey responses. Nevertheless, readers should be cautioned that our point estimates might be biased if the weighting strategy did not fully account for non-response bias.

Our concerns discussed earlier about the DEERS data resonate here as well. At the very least, DoD may want to think about ways to validate the DEERS data, e.g., through a series of brief surveys from time to time. Returning the dual-military flag to the DEERS database will also help to identify dual-military families more accurately.

The formula calculates potential need, not actual need for DoD spaces. In this document, we have emphasized the distinction between potential need, calculated by the DoD child-care demand formula, and the actual need for DoD spaces. The DoD formula, even given the concerns noted above, appears to do a reasonable job of assessing potential need for child care. But our data make clear that the formula is predicting just one child-care outcome—potential need for child care—of many outcomes. It does not speak to actual need, demand or preference for care, or use of care. As was illustrated in Figure 1.1, potential need is just one of several factors that should be considered in examining child-care outcomes and appropriate policy responses to them.

The intermediate outcomes of interest include child-care use (including multiple care arrangements); unmet need; unmet preference (assuming that a family is not using its most-preferred option); ultimate outcomes, including time lost to duty because of child-care problems; and the degree to which child care is playing any role in a military member's thinking about leaving the military. The output of the DoD formula describes potential need for child care. This output number, unencumbered by the realities of local markets, installation characteristics, or family predilections, sets an upper bound on the need for child care. It indicates how many children need care because they are young and in need of supervision, because they live with their military parent(s), or because their parents work outside the home or go to school. But our data make clear that not all families who need care will use formal care, and not all the care they use or want will be DoD-sponsored care. Our analyses also provide some insight into the factors that influence a number of child-care outcomes, including what type of child care to use, what type of child care a family might prefer, and whether child care is playing any role in a parent thinking about leaving the military.

Unmet Child-Care Need Is Not Prevalent Among Military Families

Just over 10 percent of military families reported unmet child-care need. While this percentage is low, the DoD may be concerned that it is not zero. We find that unmet need is much more prevalent among families with preschool-age children than among families with school-age children. This finding suggests that, while the DoD is understandably concerned about providing care for school-age children, the biggest gaps in meeting need continue to be in providing care to preschool-age children. Families with a civilian working spouse are more likely to express unmet need, as are families earning less than $50,000 per year. This suggests that policies that give dual-military and single-parent families a preference for DoD-sponsored care may be effective in reducing unmet need among these populations, but also that further attention is required to address the needs of military members who are married to civilians.

Unmet Preference Is More Common than Unmet Need

A larger proportion of military families—22 percent—reported unmet preference than unmet need for child care. Again, we find a greater prevalence of unmet preference among families with preschool-age children. Families have unmet preference for different types of care. Overall, 54 percent of the families who reported unmet preference stated that their preferred form of care is one that is provided by DoD. This means that nearly half of families expressing unmet preference would like something other than what DoD currently provides. This further suggests that DoD may need to develop other ways to meet the child-care preferences of military families if providing a range of options and meeting preferences is a policy concern.

Child-Care Concerns May Influence Retention Decisions

Our research confirms and expands on the findings of previous studies (cited in Chapter Four) that found that spousal employment and child-care issues are important factors in military retention. More than one-fifth of survey respondents report that it is likely or very likely that child-care issues would lead them to leave the military. It is important to emphasize that simply because individuals report that they are likely to leave the service does not mean that they will act on that stated intention. Further information would be needed to determine whether individuals who express a propensity to leave the service due to child-care issues actually do so. Nevertheless, families with preschool-age children were much more likely to report a propensity to leave the military due to child-care issues than families with school-age children. This difference may be partially due to the fact that the parents of older children tend to be older themselves and have a longer tenure in and stronger commitment to a military career.

Family status has a strong relationship to plans to leave the service. Families with a non-working civilian spouse are much less likely to express such plans. Families using CDC care, controlling for family type, are more likely to indicate that child-care issues may lead the military member to leave the military, a surprising finding in some respects, given that these families receive a large child-care subsidy and are receiving the most-preferred type of care. In other respects, it is not so surprising. A significant portion of parents using a CDC (53 percent) reported using at least one other child-care arrangement to cover duty time in the past week. And the large subsidy that CDC families receive appears to count for little. Our focus groups revealed that many CDC parents feel that CDC care costs too much. Most are unaware that they receive a subsidy, and some even believe that DoD is making a profit from the CDCs. DoD has much to gain by raising awareness of the fact that CDC care is in fact heavily subsidized and that parents' fees cover less than half of the cost of care.

Dual-Military and Single-Parent Families Face Greater Challenges

Despite the fact that DoD policy gives special priority to dual-military and single-parent families in terms of accessing DoD-sponsored child-care options, these families are much more likely than families with a military member married to a civilian to report that the military member plans to leave the military due to child-care issues.

This is true even though these families are less likely to report unmet need. This may reflect the greater challenges of raising children in the military either alone or with a military spouse, even when high-quality child care is available. It may also reflect the fact that the type of care for which single parents receive a preference (CDC care) is the least-flexible arrangement and may be least able to accommodate the demands of the military schedule. DoD may want to consider other ways to support parents, perhaps by offering and subsidizing a larger range of child-care options, including wraparound care that fills in child-care gaps, sick-child care, and subsidies for civilian care. Although DoD has mechanisms in place to reintegrate most military families into the DoD child-care system after deployment that appear to be working, single-parent families are still experiencing difficulty reentering the system post-deployment and may need additional support.

Families Living Off Base Are Less Likely to Use DoD-Sponsored Care

Families that live off base are less likely to use DoD-sponsored child-care options, and the propensity to use DoD-sponsored care decreases as the distance between a family's home and the base grows. It appears that many families that live off base do not find DoD-sponsored care, which is typically located on the installation, to be a convenient option. Nevertheless, these families do seem to be able to find other options that meet their needs. It may be the case that while DoD-sponsored care is able to meet the needs of many if not most families who live on base, those families are less attracted to off-base options if they cannot be accommodated by DoD-sponsored care. This suggests that the housing distribution of military families stationed on a particular installation is an important characteristic for the DoD to consider in deciding how to allocate its child-care resources. It may be advisable, for example, to provide subsidies or vouchers for civilian care in locations where few families live on an installation if the DoD can be assured that the quality of that care matches high DoD standards.

DoD CDC Users Appear to Have a Weaker Attachment to the Military

The conventional wisdom is that DoD CDC care is the most sought-after and convenient type of child care among military families. Certainly, waiting lists are long, and the subsidy provided to families that use this type of care is much larger than the subsidy available for any other type of care. However, our analysis reveals that, controlling for family type, families who use the DoD CDCs are more likely than families who use other care options to report that they are likely to leave the military due to child-care issues. This may be due in part to selection issues, and one should not conclude that the use of CDC care is *causing* a higher propensity to leave the military. Families that choose CDC care may differ in observed and unobservable ways that are also related to the probability of leaving the military. For example, it may be the case that the families who chose CDC care are the families who have the most difficult time balancing work and family demands. Given that DoD heavily subsidizes care provided in the CDCs, and provides little or no subsidy for other options, DoD may be interested in more fully understanding what CDC families might need in order to make balancing duty and parenting responsibilities less difficult. It would also be important to examine whether CDC families differ in unobserved ways from other families, and whether CDC staff or programs can assist families in addressing the broader child-care challenges that they face.

Local Market Conditions Are Related to the Child-Care Choices that DoD Families Make

Although DoD-sponsored care is an important option for military families, it is not the only option. Our analysis reveals that families with preschool-age children who live in areas with lower median incomes are more likely to use civilian child care than DoD-sponsored care. The relationship between median income and use of civilian child care may reflect the implications of differences in cost of living. Because the income of military families does not vary much by locale, military families who live in affluent communities may be less willing or less able than military families who live in poorer communities to pay the market price for civilian child care. This situation suggests that characteristics of the local community may be important determinants of the relative need for DoD-sponsored care. Attention to these issues may help DoD to effectively allocate its child-care resources.

Recommendations

Because the DoD child-care demand formula calculates only a single child-care outcome—potential need—the formula should be renamed. If it were called the "potential child-care need formula," it would clarify what it does and what it does not do. What the formula does is very important: It identifies an upward bound on need and, in doing so, enables planners to compare potential need (defined by the required number of child-care spaces) to the existing number of child-care spaces. This creates continuing pressure from the child-care community to acknowledge unmet potential need and attempt to meet it. But the current DoD formula does little to help policymakers allocate those spaces to best meet the needs of the military or of families with young children. Its focus on a single outcome—potential need—provides limited direction in setting policy or in guiding the allocation of constrained resources. The exclusive focus on the number of spaces that are potentially needed implicitly limits policy responses to providing those spaces within a DoD system dominated by CDCs and FCC.

It is important that DoD understand the limits of the formula and focus its efforts on local allocation strategies. Other factors that we found to be important in child-care use, such as housing patterns around an installation, could be included in the formula to provide DoD with clearer direction on the best use of child-care resources and support.

DoD should focus on other child-care outcomes in addition to potential need. Our analyses focused on several child-care outcomes that might be—and arguably should be—of concern to DoD. Child-care use, unmet need, and unmet preference are three intermediate child-care outcomes that should be of interest to the DoD. As discussed earlier, given that military child care is an employer-sponsored system, readiness and retention of military personnel should be the ultimate outcomes of most concern, and intermediate outcomes are important to the degree that they affect the ultimate outcomes. Yet, for example, little attention is paid to time lost from duty because of child-care problems in setting incentives for providers to provide particular kinds of care or in allocating resources to help families meet their needs, even though these items would presumably be very important DoD priorities.

One approach to reducing time lost from duty due to child-care issues might be to encourage a more responsive FCC provider system on local installations. While FCC providers who offer part-day care certainly can serve some families, such providers are not optimizing FCC's potential value to DoD. DoD might consider providing incentives to FCC providers that agree to be available during regular duty hours and that are willing to provide additional care in a flexible manner. Such incentives would be consistent with the current use of incentives to FCC providers that further other DoD goals, such as providing infant or special-needs care. Once such FCC providers are in place, DoD could then offer incentives to those types of families that our analyses identified as being most in need of supplemental care to encourage those families to use the providers that offer the care.

Our analyses also indicate that the enrollment priority and large subsidies that single-parent and dual-military families are receiving in CDCs are not advancing DoD's purported goals of readiness and retention; the CDCs' understandably limited hours are forcing these families to locate, negotiate, and pay for additional child care that covers their duty time. At the same time, if a DoD goal is to maximize parental choice and provide maximum autonomy for providers in what they offer, such incentives might not be an appropriate use of limited resources.

DoD needs to identify and prioritize key intermediate outcomes and then follow those outcomes to the desired conclusions indicated in this analysis. This sort of prioritization would help DoD to determine how to allocate limited child-care resources within a system defined by the potential need formula.

DoD should recognize the limits of the child-care demand formula and consider the local factors that influence child-care outcomes in formulating policy responses. The current child-care demand formula currently does not take into account key characteristics that our data indicate have an impact on multiple child-care outcomes, including child-care use and child-care preferences. According to the formula, two installations with the same number of children age 5 and under, the same distribution of dual-military and single-parent families, and the same number of spouses working outside the home would exhibit the same level of potential child-care need. But our data show that characteristics of an installation influence how potential need translates into use of DoD-sponsored care.

For example, because families who live on or near an installation are more inclined to use DoD-sponsored CDCs and FCC on base and prefer to use those types of care, an installation with limited on- and near-base housing is likely to face lower actual need for on-base child care. To address unmet need on such installations, the DoD should consider subsidizing child-care spaces in civilian centers in those communities where military families actually live. Analogously, in communities with a low cost of living, families may prefer civilian care because it is cheaper for most of them. In those communities, subsidizing spaces might not be the best use of resources. Instead, to address unmet need in those communities, DoD might consider subsidizing wraparound care that will fill in the child-care gaps for families whose duty hours extend beyond the operating hours of civilian centers so that parents can avoid missing duty.

It would be useful for DoD to clarify which outcomes are of greatest concern and should drive the child-care system. While it is unlikely that DoD will ever reach a point at which it could supply enough spaces to meet the upper bound of potential child-care need, as defined by the DoD formula, it is nevertheless worthwhile to think about optimal system outcomes in order to allocate resources in the most effective way. For example, one goal might be to reduce the level of unmet preference as much as possible. Another might be to reduce the level of unmet need. Still another might be to reduce the number of duty days missed by military personnel due to child-care problems.

These outcomes may have very different implications for system policies and the use of limited resources.

A major difficulty in thinking about desired outcomes is that, currently, DoD has few policy levers in the child-care arena. The key policy lever is the number of spaces available for care in DoD-sponsored child-care settings. However, this lever is not completely under the control of DoD child-care policymakers. The decision to build a new child-care center is made at the local level by the installation commander, and there are many good reasons why this decision is a local one. However, a base commander's decision on whether to build a new CDC is often made within a context in which many demands are placed on military construction (MILCON) funds and other funds, making unmet need for child care only a minor issue. In contrast, expansion of FCC programs is often constrained not by lack of funding but by the lack of potential providers. More incentives to FCC providers, which could range from higher subsidies to backup support, might increase the number of military dependents willing to provide FCC in their homes.

If DoD wants more control over child-care outcomes, it would be advised to create more policy alternatives in the child-care arena. Those alternatives might include child-care vouchers, subsidized spaces in civilian centers, subsidized wraparound care, and support for after-school programs in the community. Some of these alternatives have been promulgated by the individual military services, but the services have not had much impact at the system level. Recently, however, DoD introduced a new program called "Operation: Military Child Care" that will help active duty, reserve, and National Guard families that do not have access to DoD-sponsored care on base to locate child care. The program will also defray the cost of that care while military members of those families are mobilized or deployed. This program is specifically targeted at families that do not have access to DoD options and that may be experiencing increased need for child care. But, as our data show, many families that do have access to DoD-sponsored care actually prefer other options, so this program may have broader appeal than just to those who do not have access to care on base. The policies developed under this new program may help to create a wider array of child-care options for all military families.

DoD should collect additional data to improve the formula and better target child-care resources. The DoD potential need formula relies on DEERS data to determine the distribution of family types, a key component in the calculation of potential need. But our analyses raise questions about the accuracy of those data. It would be advisable for DoD to conduct small validation studies of the DEERS data and, if indicated, consider ways to improve the data's quality, e.g., by providing increased incentives for military members to report changes in their family status.

We strongly urge that DoD reinstate the dual-military flag in the DEERS database. This analytic category is difficult and time-consuming to create, and its accuracy is unacceptably low. It would be far more efficient to recreate the flag and to use the dual-military flag itself in the validation studies recommended above.

In applying the potential need formula at the installation level, it is important to collect and utilize data on housing patterns and local market conditions. Data on neither of these critical contributors to child-care use are currently collected, yet our analysis clearly indicates that they are significant contributors to a family's decisions about child-care use. Easy access to this information would allow policymakers to improve the targeting of local child-care resources.

Our analyses indicate that CDC users are those who are *most* likely to be considering leaving the military, despite receiving the most heavily subsidized and generally most-desired child care. It would be very worthwhile for DoD to know the reasons for this pattern. Is it that center-based care simply cannot meet all of a family's child-care needs, and the search for and use of additional care is costly and disruptive? Is it that the long duty hours of military parents limit the support that the military member can provide to his or her family? Is it that these families do not know how large a subsidy they are receiving? Or is it that younger families have other child-related issues that no CDC can address, such as gaps in sick-child care, a lack of money for supplemental care or for babysitting, or difficulties reconciling the responsibilities of military duty with the responsibilities of rearing young children?

Finally, we urge DoD to include questions on child-care issues on the survey given to personnel leaving the military. The more that DoD learns about the role that child care plays in the critical decision to stay in or leave the military, the better that child-care resources can be targeted to meet critical needs.

A DoD-wide role may be needed to allocate child-care resources effectively. Our survey results suggest that there is no one-size-fits-all approach that can effectively address the child-care needs of DoD families. The survey results also suggest that potential need, as characterized by the DoD formula, can best be met with a range of child-care options. While the formula provides a useful starting point for predicting child-care need, installation characteristics, in particular the average income of the local community and the housing decisions of military families, appear to have important implications for the type of care used and the need for DoD-operated child-care spaces as opposed to other options, such as subsidized care in the community.

Currently, there is no mechanism for the centralized determination of child-care needs across installations. Individual commanders, or in some cases the services, decide how to allocate funding for the construction and operation of CDCs. This leads to tremendous variation in the level of child-care availability across installations. Higher-level consideration of child-care needs across installations, combined with the use of a broader set of policy tools, could lead to more options that would promote the military's ultimate goals: readiness and retention.

Clearer DoD directives concerning key child-care goals based on better data, combined with a package of policy options that extend beyond creating spaces in DoD-sponsored care, will help DoD to better allocate child-care resources. More options that are better targeted will promote DoD's goals and provide families with more child-care choices. Better targeting would also increase parent satisfaction.

DoD has built a system that strives to meet the needs of the military as well as the needs of parents and children through the provision of high-quality care in a range of settings. The potential need formula is a useful tool for identifying need. But it provides little help in targeting resources. New data collection, a focus on multiple outcomes, and expanded policy options will help DoD to better meet its own goals and families' child-care needs.

APPENDIX A

Components of the Child-Care Need Formula: DoD and the Military Services

This appendix provides an overview of how the individual services have adapted the DoD child-care demand formula. Table A.1 lists the calculations that the services use to estimate child-care need.

For Children Age 0–5

Children of Single Parents

All the services use the same percentage, multiplied by the total number of children age 0–5, that DoD uses (8 percent) to calculate the number of children of single parents, except for the Air Force, which uses a slightly lower number (6 percent).

Children of Dual-Military Couples

All the services, except the Army, use a higher percentage than DoD uses to calculate the number of children of dual-military couples. The Marine Corps and Navy both use 6 percent, and the Air Force uses 8 percent, while DoD and the Army use 4 percent.

Children of Military Married to Civilians

From the information we have, the Air Force, Army, and Marine Corps calculate the number of children of military personnel married to civilians in the same way that DoD calculates it (multiplying the total number of children by 88 percent). The Navy does not estimate the number of children in military-married-to civilian families separately.

Table A.1
Child-Care Demand Formulas Used by the Services

Categories of Child-Care Users	Air Force	Army	Marine Corps	Navy
(1) Children age 0–5	N/A	N/A	N/A	N/A
(2) Children of single parents [a]	(1) x 0.06 x 0.90	(1) x 0.08 x 0.90	(1) x 0.08 x 0.97	(1) x 0.08 x 0.90
(3) Children of dual-military couples [b]	(1) x 0.08 x 0.85	(1) x 0.04 x 0.85	(1) x 0.06 x 0.88	(1) x 0.06 x 0.85
(4) Children of military married to civilians [c]	(1) x 0.88 x 0.90	(1) x 0.88 x 0.90	(1) x 0.88 x 0.80	N/A
(5) Children of spouses working full time [d]	(4) x 0.43 x 0.60	(4) x 0.43 x 0.60	(4) x 0.43 x 0.60	(4) x 0.86 x 0.90 x 0.54 x 0.059 [e]
(6) Children of spouses working part time [f]	(4) x 0.43 x 0.40 x 0.50	(4) x 0.43 x 0.40 x 0.50	(4) x 0.43 x 0.40 x 0.50	(4) x 0.86 x 0.90 x 0.54 x 0.41 x 0.50 [g]
(7) Civilian need for child-care spaces	Total number of civilians x 0.03	Total number of civilians x 0.025	Total number of civilians x 0.0125	Total number of civilians x 0.0125
(8) Unaccompanied tours	Reduction	N/A	N/A	N/A
(9) Do not want care on base	Reduction	N/A	N/A	N/A

Table A.1—Continued

Categories of Child-Care Users	Air Force	Army	Marine Corps	Navy
(10) Reduction in force	Reduction	N/A	N/A	Total number of spaces needed x 0.82
(11) Total number of spaces needed	(2) + (3) + (5) + (6) + (7) – (8) – (9) – (10)	(2) + (3) + (5) + (6) + (7)	(2) + (3) + (5) + (6) + (7)	(2) + (3) + (5) + (6) + (7) x 0.82 x 0.65 [h]

[a] Number of children 0–5 x percentage of children 0–5 of single parents x percentage of children living with their parents.

[b] Number of children 0–5 x percentage of children 0–5 of dual-military couples x percentage of children living with their parents.

[c] Number of children 0–5 x percentage of children 0–5 of military married to civilian x percentage of children living with their parents.

[d] Number of children of military married to civilians x percentage of civilian parents employed outside the home x percentage employed full time (note: for all services except the Navy).

[e] Number of children of military married to civilians x percentage of children living with their parents (excluding children of single parents and dual-military couples) x percentage of spouses employed outside the home x percentage of spouses working full time.

[F] Number of children of military married to civilians x percentage of children of single parents x percentage employed part time x 1/2 space for each (note: for all services except the Navy).

[g] Number of children of military married to civilians x children living with their parents (excluding children of single parents and dual-military couples) x percentage of spouses employed outside the home x percentage of spouses working part time x 1/2 space for each.

[h] The Navy's goal is to meet 65 percent of the need.

NOTE: N/A = not applicable.

Children of Spouses Working Full Time

The Army, Air Force, and Marine Corps all calculate the number of children of civilian spouses working full time in the same way that DoD calculates it (60 percent). The Navy estimates this number somewhat differently by excluding children of single-parent and dual-military couples when calculating the number of children with both parents working full time (therefore, in effect, estimating the number of children of military married to civilians). The Navy also uses a higher percentage (54 percent) in estimating the number of spouses employed outside the home compared with the percentage (43 percent) used by DoD and the other services, and the Navy uses a slightly lower percentage (59 percent) to estimate the number of spouses working full time than the percentage DoD and the other services use (60 percent).

Children of Spouses Working Part Time

Again, except for the Navy, all the services calculate the number of children of spouses working part time in the same way that DoD calculates it (40 percent). The Navy excludes children in single-parent and dual-military families, and it uses a higher number (54 percent) than DoD uses (43 percent) to estimate the number of spouses employed outside the home and the number of spouses working part time (41 percent versus DoD's 40 percent).

Children of DoD-Employed Civilians

The Marine Corps and Navy use the same percentage that DoD uses (1.25 percent) to estimate civilian need for DoD-sponsored child care, while the Army and Air Force use higher percentages (2.5 percent and 3 percent, respectively).

Other Differences Among the Services' Formulas

The Air Force makes reductions in its child-care need estimates by taking into account military parents on unaccompanied tours and those families who do not want care on base. The Navy takes into account reduction in force (the estimated total number of child-care spaces, multiplied by 82 percent) and its goal of meeting 65 percent of the child-care need into its final potential need estimate.

In addition to the factors included in the DoD child-care formula described above, OSD has encouraged the services to take into account several other factors that may affect the number of child-care spaces required by military families:

- Number of military from all services assigned to an installation
- Number of civilians working on base not married to military personnel
- Age, rank, and marital status of the military population
- Anticipated changes in the size of military and civilian populations (due to deployments, downsizing, etc.)
- Family housing plans (e.g., renovations, new construction)
- High cost and/or poor quality of off-base civilian child care; location of off-base civilian child care
- Other factors that would contribute to reduced need for child care: civilian community child-care centers offering care at comparable or lower costs, availability of HeadStart programs, reputation of on-base care
- Number of children age 0–5 living on and off the base.

For Children Age 6–12

The formulas used by the services to determine child-care need for children age 6–12 years are more similar to one another than the formulas used by the services to determine need for children in the 0–5 age group. A major difference between how DoD and the services calculate need for 6- to 12-year-olds is shown in the formula used by the Navy and Air Force for estimating the number of children with parents working full time or part time. Both services use percentages that are smaller than the percentage used by DoD for estimating the number of spouses employed outside the home and the number of spouses working full time, and they use higher percentages than DoD to estimate the number of parents working part time. The most notable difference between the DoD formula and the Navy's estimates of need is in the percentage used to calculate the number of children of parents working full time and part time, which differs by 20 percentage points.

The Air Force factors in reductions in need due to military personnel on unaccompanied tours, families who do not want care on base, and the number of children living on base, and it factors in a reduction for children 10 to 12 years old (because many of those children do not attend school-age care programs).

DoD, the Marine Corps, and the Navy multiply the total need count by 0.33 to estimate the amount of need on base.

APPENDIX B
Military Child Care Survey

The following pages of this appendix contain the military child care survey sent to a sample of 3,000 families of active duty military members. The survey asked parents about their child-care arrangements, unmet needs for care, unmet preferences for care, and the effect of child-care issues on their readiness and intention to remain in the military. The findings and recommendations in this document are based on the survey results and on focus groups with military parents.

CARD 01 5-6/

RCS-DD-P&R(OT)2168

1-4/ Expiration: 10/31/2006

DATE RCVD: [ ] [ ] [ ] [ ] [ ] [ ] 7-12/ BATCH [ ] [ ] [ ] [ ] 13-16/

MILITARY CHILD CARE SURVEY

17/

This questionnaire is to be filled out by either or both parents about the child whose name appears on the label.

If this child does NOT live with you AND you do not participate in any child care decisions, please check here and return this survey in the enclosed self-addressed envelope: [ ]

→

Child's Name

Child's Age

RAND Corporation, 1700 Main St., P.O. Box 2138
Santa Monica, CA 90407-2138

Rev 2/19/2004

ABOUT THIS QUESTIONNAIRE

PURPOSE

- The purpose of this survey is to help the Services better understand service members' child care needs, preferences, and problems.
- This survey, being fielded by the RAND Corporation, a nonprofit research institution in Santa Monica, California, and supported by the Office of the Secretary of Defense, is being conducted in coordination with the Army, Air Force, Navy, and Marine Corps and the Defense Manpower Data Center (DMDC) of the Department of Defense.

WHY SHOULD I BOTHER?

- You have been selected at random to represent a larger group of military parents in all four Services. We will combine your responses with the responses of other parents to draw conclusions about the views and experiences of parents overall. We need responses from all types of parents—single parents, dual military parents, as well as military members with civilian spouses.
- While no decisions about you alone will be made based on this survey, survey results will influence policy discussions and may result in changes that affect you as well as other military parents. **If you don't respond, your views and the views of other parents like you will not be considered in military child care policy reviews and changes.**

WILL MY SURVEY RESPONSES BE KEPT PRIVATE?

- YES. **RAND and DMDC will treat your answers as strictly confidential.** Your responses will be combined with information from many other members to report the views and experiences of different types of military parents. Comments may be reported word for word, but never with identifiable information.
- **RAND and DMDC will not release data that could identify you to anyone.** No supervisors or other officials will see your questionnaire, nor will RAND or DMDC release any data that could identify you to anyone in your Service, other Department of Defense agencies, or anyone else, except as required by law.
- We may combine your survey responses with information provided to us by the Department of Defense from your administrative files, such as your military occupational specialty, your duty assignments, your reenlistment status, and so forth. We may also request your participation in a follow-up survey at a future date.
- This study is completely voluntary. There is no penalty if you choose not to respond. However, RAND and the Department of Defense strongly encourage you to participate. If you prefer not to answer a specific questions for any reason, you may just leave it blank.

PRIVACY NOTICE

In accordance with the Privacy Act of 1974 (Public Law 93-579), this notice informs you of the purpose of the survey and how findings will be used. Please read it carefully.

AUTHORITY: 10 United States Code, Sections 136, 1782 and 2358.

PRINCIPAL PURPOSE: Information collected in this survey will be used to assist in formulating policies that affect personnel management, retention, and quality of life for enlisted service members. Reports will be provided to the Secretary of Defense, each Military Service, and the Joint Chiefs of Staff. Results will be used in reports and testimony provided to Congress. Some results may be published by RAND, the Defense Manpower Data Center (DMDC) or professional journals, or reported in manuscripts presented at conferences, symposia, and scientific meetings. In no case will the data be reported or used to identify individual respondents.

DISCLOSURE: Your participation in this survey is voluntary. There is no penalty if you choose not to respond. However, maximum participation is encouraged so that the data will be complete and representative. Your survey instrument will be treated as confidential. Identifying information will be used only by persons engaged in, and for purposes of, the survey research. Only group statistics will be published.

ROUTINE USES: None.

The first group of questions is about the CHILD whose name appears on the survey cover.

- If this child is school-aged and the child's school was in session LAST WEEK, please refer to the child care arrangements you used last week in answering Question 1 about a typical week.
- If this child's school was NOT in session last week, please refer to the LAST WEEK your child's school WAS in session in answering Question 1 about a typical week.

Section 1: Your Child Care Arrangements

1. What child care arrangement do you use the most hours in a typical week during the hours you and/or your spouse are working or attending school? ***(If you use more than one source of child care for this child, please check the ONE you use the MOST.)***

(Check One) *18-19/*

DoD Programs:

☐1 DoD child development center

☐2 DoD home or family child care (FCC)

☐3 DoD school age care program

☐4 DoD youth center

☐5 DoD before or after-school program

Civilian Programs:

☐6 Civilian before or after-school program

☐7 Civilian child care center

☐8 Civilian family child care

Parent or Relative Care:

☐9 Relative in your home

☐10 Relative outside your home

☐11 Care provided by mother

☐12 Care provided by father

☐13 Older sister or brother takes care of child

☐14 Child takes care of himself or herself

Other:

☐15 Non-relative in your home

☐16 Non-relative outside your home

☐17 Other (Specify):

______________________________ *20/*

2. How would you rate the quality of care of the child care arrangement you checked in Question 1?

(Check One) *21/*

☐1 Excellent

☐2 Very good

☐3 Good

☐4 Fair

☐5 Poor

CARD 01

3. LAST WEEK, how many hours did you use the child care arrangement you listed in Question 1?

[| |] Number of hours 22-24/

4. What was the cost of the child care you listed in Question 1 LAST WEEK or the MOST RECENT WEEK you used it for this child?

$ [| |] ***(Round to the Nearest Dollar; Enter 0 if you don't pay)*** 25-27/

5. Using the list below, what were the **FIVE MOST IMPORTANT THINGS** you considered in choosing the child care arrangement you use for the most hours per week? (This is the arrangement you checked in Question 1.)

Logistics:
- 01. Transportation available
- 02. Cost
- 03. Hours of operation
- 04. Location/convenience
- 05. Provider could take my child immediately
- 06. Provider could accommodate all my children
- 07. Ease of monitoring provider

Nature of Care:
- 08. Age ranges of other children
- 09. Available activities
- 10. Cleanliness
- 11. Quality of facilities & equipment
- 12. Academic or school readiness focus
- 13. Developmental focus

Provider:
- 14. Child/staff ratio
- 15. Family environment
- 16. Religious or cultural environment
- 17. Familiarity or comfort with provider
- 18. Provider's philosophy
- 19. Level of supervision
- 20. Reliability of care

Other: (Please Specify Below):
- 21. ______________________ 28/

____

____

Please enter codes in the boxes below for UP TO FIVE things.

[|] 1st Most Important 29-30/

[|] 2nd Most Important 31-32/

[|] 3rd Most Important 33-34/

[|] 4th Most Important 35-36/

[|] 5th Most Important 37-38/

CARD 01

6. How satisfied overall are you with the arrangement you checked in Question 1?

(Check One) 39/

- ☐1 Very satisfied
- ☐2 Satisfied
- ☐3 Not completely satisfied
- ☐4 Dissatisfied
- ☐5 Very Dissatisfied

7. If less than very satisfied, what problems do you have with this arrangement? PLEASE PRINT CLEARLY.

______________________________ 40/

____

____

____

8. Thinking about the child care arrangement you checked in Question 1, would you prefer another arrangement?

(Check One) 41/

- ☐1 Yes
- ☐2 No → ***Skip to Question 11, Next Page***

9. If yes, what other child care arrangement would you MOST prefer?

(Check One) 42-43/

DoD Programs:

- ☐1 DoD child development center
- ☐2 DoD home or family child care (FCC)
- ☐3 DoD school age care program
- ☐4 DoD youth center
- ☐5 DoD before or after-school program

Civilian Programs:

- ☐6 Civilian before or after-school program
- ☐7 Civilian child care center
- ☐8 Civilian family child care

Parent or Relative Care:

- ☐9 Relative in your home
- ☐10 Relative outside your home
- ☐11 Care provided by mother
- ☐12 Care provided by father
- ☐13 Older sister or brother takes care of child
- ☐14 Child takes care of himself or herself

Other:

- ☐15 Non-relative in your home
- ☐16 Non-relative outside your home
- ☐17 Other (Specify):

______________________________ 44/

CARD 01

10. What stops you from using this preferred arrangement for this particular child?

(Check All That Apply)

- ☐1 Too expensive 45/
- ☐2 Hours not convenient 46/
- ☐3 Location not convenient 47/
- ☐4 Quality not high enough 48/
- ☐5 Lack of availability / No openings right now 49/
- ☐6 Provider can't accommodate my other children 50/
- ☐7 Preferred caretaker (self, relative, sibling) not available to provide care 51/
- ☐8 No reason / No other 52/
- ☐9 Other (Please Specify): ______________________________ 53/ 54/

11. LAST WEEK, did you use other child care arrangements for this child in addition to the one listed in Question 1? *(Include extra care for weekend work or for 24-hour care, e.g., overnight stays)*

(Check One) 55/

- ☐1 Yes
- ☐2 No → ***Skip to Question 17, Next Page***

12. Please check the **additional** child care arrangements you used for this particular child LAST WEEK.

(Check All That Apply)

DoD Programs:

- ☐1 DoD child development center 56/
- ☐2 DoD home or family child care (FCC) 57/
- ☐3 DoD school age care program 58/
- ☐4 DoD youth center 59/
- ☐5 DoD before or after-school program 60/

Civilian Programs:

- ☐6 Civilian before or after-school program 61/
- ☐7 Civilian child care center 62/
- ☐8 Civilian family child care 63/

Parent or Relative Care:

- ☐9 Relative in your home 64/
- ☐10 Relative outside your home 65-66/
- ☐11 Care provided by mother 67-68/
- ☐12 Care provided by father 69-70/
- ☐13 Older sister or brother takes care of child 71-72/
- ☐14 Child takes care of himself or herself 73-74/

Other:

- ☐15 Non-relative in your home 75-76/
- ☐16 Non-relative outside your home 77-78/
- ☐17 Other (Specify): 79-80/

______________________________ 81/

CARD 01

CARD 02 5-6/

1-4/

13. How would you rate the average quality of care of the child care arrangements you checked in Question 12?

(Check One) 7/

- ☐1 Excellent
- ☐2 Very good
- ☐3 Good
- ☐4 Fair
- ☐5 Poor

14. Enter the number of hours you used the **additional** child care arrangements you listed in Question 12 LAST WEEK.

☐☐ Number of hours 8-9/

15. Enter the cost of the **additional** child care arrangements you listed in Question 12 for this child LAST WEEK.

$ ☐☐☐ ***(Round to the nearest dollar; Enter 0 if you don't pay)*** 10-12/

16. Why did you need more than one child care arrangement for this child LAST WEEK?

(Check All That Apply)

- ☐1 My spouse or I worked the night shift 13/
- ☐2 My spouse or I worked a 24-hour shift 14/
- ☐3 My spouse or I worked weekends 15/
- ☐4 My spouse or I worked extended hours 16/
- ☐5 Unexpected child care need (e.g., child ill, regular care not available, family emergency, school closure) 17/
- ☐6 My spouse or I attended school 18/
- ☐7 Other reason (Please Explain): ______________________________ 19/ 20/

17. How long did it take you to find care for the child whose name appears on the survey cover? ***(Please answer a and b)***

a. After this child was first born (Include search time during pregnancy)

☐☐ Number of Days, OR 21-22/
☐☐ Number of Weeks, OR 23-24/
☐☐ Number of Months 25-26/

☐1 Not applicable (did not need care after the birth) 27/

b. When you first moved to this installation

☐☐ Number of Days, OR 28-29/
☐☐ Number of Weeks, OR 30-31/
☐☐ Number of Months 32-33/

☐1 Not applicable 34/ (child was born after I arrived at this installation)

18. Did lack of child care after the birth of your child or when you first moved to this installation keep you or your spouse from:

(Check All That Apply)

- ☐1 Looking for civilian work 35/
- ☐2 Beginning a civilian job 36/
- ☐3 Reporting for military duty 37/
- ☐4 Attending school 38/
- ☐5 None of the above 39/

19. After you found care, did you remain on a waiting list for other preferred child care for this child?

(Check One) 40/

- ☐1 Yes
- ☐2 No → ***Skip to Question 20***

19a. If yes, how long did it take you to find a child care arrangement that you were comfortable with?

☐☐ # of Days 41-42/ OR ☐☐ # of Weeks 43-44/ OR ☐☐ # of Months 45-46/

20. Thinking about the future, how likely is it that child care issues would lead your family to leave the military?

(Check One) 47/

- ☐1 Very likely
- ☐2 Somewhat likely
- ☐3 Neither likely or unlikely
- ☐4 Somewhat unlikely
- ☐5 Very unlikely

21. To what extent have child care issues had a negative effect on you and your spouse's career advancement and/or affected your choice of assignments?

(Circle one number from 1-6 for each military member and civilian spouse)

	To a Very Great Extent	To a Great Extent	To Some Extent	To a Very Little Extent	Not At All	Not Applicable	
a. Military Member **(FATHER)**:	1	2	3	4	5	6	48/
b. Military Member **(MOTHER)**:	1	2	3	4	5	6	49/
c. Civilian spouse:	1	2	3	4	5	6	50/

CARD 02

Please explain your responses to Questions 20 and 21. PLEASE PRINT CLEARLY. 51/

____

____

____

____

____

22. Does anyone other than the child's parents or step-parents regularly care for the child?

(Check One) 52/

- ☐1 Yes → ***Skip to Question 25, Next Page***
- ☐2 No

23. Why don't you use formal child care arrangements for this child?

____ 53/

____

____

24. How do you manage without using any type of formal child care for this child?

(Check All That Apply)

- ☐1 My spouse or I have flexible work schedules. 54/
- ☐2 My spouse and I work different shifts. 55/
- ☐3 One spouse is not working outside the home. 56/
- ☐4 My child is old enough to take care of himself or herself. 57/
- ☐5 My child has older brothers or sisters who can take care of him/her. 58/
- ☐6 One parent is self-employed and works at home. 59/
- ☐7 Other reason (Please Describe): ______________________________ 60/

____ 61/

____

____

____

CARD 02

Section 2: Most Recent Deployment

25. As a result of the most recent deployment of a military parent for more than 30 days, did your child care arrangement change for the child whose name appears on the survey cover?

(Check One) 62/

- ☐1 Yes
- ☐2 No ➔ ***Skip to Question 29, Next Page***
- ☐3 Not applicable / Never deployed ➔ ***Skip to Question 29, Next Page***

26. How did your child care arrangement change for this child?

(Check All That Apply)

- ☐1 Withdrew from the DoD system 63/
- ☐2 Withdrew from non-DoD care arrangement 64/
- ☐3 Arranged for more care 65/
- ☐4 Civilian spouse left labor force or changed jobs 66/
- ☐5 Child moved elsewhere 67/
- ☐6 Other (Please Specify): ______________________ 68/ 69/

27. When the most-recent deployment ended, did you try to return to your pre-deployment child care arrangement?

(Check One) 70/

- ☐1 Yes
- ☐2 No

28. When the most-recent deployment ended, how difficult was it to get the child care you needed for the child whose name appears on the survey cover?

(Check One) 71/

- ☐1 Very difficult
- ☐2 Difficult
- ☐3 Somewhat difficult
- ☐4 A little difficult
- ☐5 Not at all difficult

CARD 02

Section 3: Your Family Situation

29. What best describes your family situation?

(Check One) 72/

- ☐1 Single military parent → ***Skip to Question 37, Page 11***
- ☐2 Dual military parents → ***Skip to Question 37, Page 11***
- ☐3 Military member, civilian spouse including retired military → ***Answer Questions 30-36 below***

30. What is the highest educational attainment of the **civilian spouse**?

(Check One) 73/

- ☐1 No high school diploma or equivalent
- ☐2 High school diploma or GED
- ☐3 Some college
- ☐4 AA degree
- ☐5 Bachelor's degree
- ☐6 More than college degree

31. Which of the following best describes the employment status of the **civilian spouse**?

(Check All That Apply)

- ☐1 Full-time employment outside the home 74/
- ☐2 Part-time employment outside the home 75/
- ☐3 Full-time student 76/
- ☐4 Part-time student 77/
- ☐5 Self-employed/working from home 78/
- ☐6 Family or home child care provider 79/
- ☐7 Looking for work 80/
- ☐8 Not employed outside the home 81/
- ☐9 Retired 82/

32. How many hours per week does the **civilian spouse** work or attend classes?

☐☐☐ Number of hours ***(Enter 0 if neither working nor attending school)*** 83-85/

CARD 02

CARD 03 5-6/

1-4/

THESE QUESTIONS SHOULD BE ANSWERED IF THE FAMILY INCLUDES A CIVILIAN SPOUSE. OTHERS SKIP TO QUESTION 37, PAGE 11

33. Does the **civilian spouse** usually work or attend classes the same or fixed hours every week, or does his/her hours vary from week to week, such as rotating from days to evenings or nights? ***(If the civilian spouse has more than one job, please answer for the job where he/she works the most hours.)***

(Check One) 7/

- ☐1 Fixed/same hours
- ☐2 Hours vary from week to week
- ☐3 Don't know ☐4 Not applicable (not working)

34. Where does the **civilian spouse** work for the most hours per week?

(Check One) 8/

- ☐1 At the child development center on base
- ☐2 Other job on base
- ☐3 Off base
- ☐4 At home as a family or home child care provider
- ☐5 Self-employed in another business
- ☐6 Other (Please Specify): ______________________ 9/
- ☐7 Not applicable (attending school or not working)

35. If the **civilian spouse** is not employed outside the home or attending school full-time, is it due to lack of child care options? 10/

- ☐1 Yes
- ☐2 No
- ☐3 Not applicable, civilian spouse is employed or in school full-time

36. Please tell us if you agree or disagree with the following statements about **civilian spouse** employment.

(Circle one number from 1-5 for each statement)

	Strongly Agree	Agree	Neither Agree or Disagree	Disagree	Strongly Disagree	
a. Job opportunities in the local area are limited.	1	2	3	4	5	11/
b. Better paying jobs require a long commute.	1	2	3	4	5	12/
c. Job opportunities in the local area do not make use of the skills of the civilian spouse.	1	2	3	4	5	13/

Section 4: For All Families

37. Do(es) the military parent(s) have a **civilian** job in addition to the military job? ***(If dual military parents, record answer for both the father and the mother.)***

   a. Military Member **(FATHER):** ☐1 Yes ☐2 No ☐3 Not Applicable / Father not in the military *14/*

   b. Military Member **(MOTHER):** ☐1 Yes ☐2 No ☐3 Not Applicable / Mother not in the military *15/*

38. In total, **including both military and any paid civilian work**, how many hours do(es) the military parent(s) work during a normal WEEK? If none, enter "0" in the boxes for that parent.

   a. Military Member **(FATHER):** ☐☐☐ Number of hours per week on military & civilian jobs *16-18/*
   ☐1 Not Applicable / Father not in military *19/*

   b. Military Member **(MOTHER):** ☐☐☐ Number of hours per week on military & civilian jobs *20-22/*
   ☐1 Not Applicable / Mother not in military *23/*

39. Are these hours worked the same every week or do they vary from week to week?

   a. Military Member **(FATHER):** ☐1 Hours the same every week *24/*
   ☐2 Hours vary from week to week
   ☐3 Not Applicable / Father not in military

   b. Military Member **(MOTHER):** ☐1 Hours the same every week *25/*
   ☐2 Hours vary from week to week
   ☐3 Not Applicable / Mother not in military

40. In the LAST FOUR WEEKS, how many times did a parent **arrive late for work or leave early** because of a problem with your child care arrangement (e.g., a sick child or an unscheduled school closure) for the child whose name appears on the survey cover? ***(Answer separately for each military member and civilian spouse.)***

   a. Military Member **(FATHER)** was late for work or left early due to child care problems:
   ☐☐ # times in past 4 weeks *26-27/* OR ☐1 Not Applicable / Father not in the military *28/*

   b. Military Member **(MOTHER)** was late for work or left early due to child care problems:
   ☐☐ # times in past 4 weeks *29-30/* OR ☐1 Not Applicable / Mother not in the military *31/*

   c. **Civilian Spouse** was late for work or left early due to child care problems:
   ☐☐ # times in past 4 weeks *32-33/* OR ☐1 Not Applicable / Don't have a civilian spouse or spouse does not work *34/*

CARD 03

41. In the LAST FOUR WEEKS, did any family member miss at least a day of work or school because of a problem with your child care arrangement (including unscheduled school closure) for the child whose name appears on the survey cover? ***(Answer separately for each military member and civilian spouse.)***

a. Military Member **(FATHER):** ☐1 Yes ☐2 No ☐3 Not Applicable / father not in military *35/*

b. Military Member **(MOTHER):** ☐1 Yes ☐2 No ☐3 Not Applicable / mother not in military *36/*

c. Civilian Spouse: ☐1 Yes ☐2 No ☐3 Not Applicable / no civilian spouse *37/*

42. Who cared for the child whose name appears on the survey cover the last time your regular child care was not available?

(Check All That Apply)

☐1 Does not apply; never happened *38/*
☐2 Military member stayed or went home *39/*
☐3 Civilian spouse stayed or went home *40/*
☐4 Military member (mother or father) took child to work *41/*
☐5 Civilian spouse took child to work *42/*
☐6 Relative watched child *43/*
☐7 Neighbor or friend watched child *44/*
☐8 Child watched self *45/*
☐9 Hired sitter *46/*
☐10 Older child stayed home *47-48/*
☐11 Regular provider arranged for substitute care *49-50/*
☐12 Other (Please Specify): ______________________ *51-52/* *53/*
☐13 Don't know *54-55/*

43. In the last four weeks, was the child whose name appears on the survey cover ever sick on a work day?

☐1 Yes *56/*
☐2 No

CARD 03

44. What did you do the last time this child was sick on a work or school day?

(Check All That Apply)

- ☐1 Took child to regular arrangement 57/
- ☐2 Took child to provider who accepts sick children 58/
- ☐3 Military member stayed or went home 59/
- ☐4 Civilian spouse stayed or went home 60/
- ☐5 Military member took child to work 61/
- ☐6 Civilian spouse took child to work 62/
- ☐7 Relative watched child 63/
- ☐8 Neighbor/friend watched child 64/
- ☐9 Child watched self 65/
- ☐10 Hired sitter 66-67/
- ☐11 Older child stayed home 68-69/
- ☐12 Other (Please Specify): ______________________ 70-71/ 72/
- ☐13 Don't know 73-74/

45. Do you live on a military installation?

(Check One) 75/

- ☐1 Yes → ***Skip to Question 48, Next Page***
- ☐2 No

46. If no, approximately how far away from the installation do you live?

☐☐☐ Miles 76-78/

47. Why do you live off of the military installation?

(Check All That Apply)

- ☐1 No on-base family housing available 79/
- ☐2 Spousal employment 80/
- ☐3 Housing is cheaper 81/
- ☐4 Housing is better quality 82/
- ☐5 Wanted to purchase a home 83/
- ☐6 Community characteristics (e.g., better schools) 84/
- ☐7 Other (Please Specify): ______________________ 85/ 86/

CARD 03

CARD 04 5-6/

1-4/

48. How many children are living with you now?

(***Please answer for the most recent or current accompanied tour.***)

☐☐ Number of children 7-8/

49. Please list the first name (or initials) AND date of birth of each of your dependents age 18 and under and indicate whether this child lives with you. Start with the child who is listed on the cover of this questionnaire.

	First name or initials	Lives with you YES	Lives with you NO		Date of Birth (MM/DD/YYYY)	
a.	______	☐1	☐2	9/	☐☐/☐☐/☐☐☐☐	10-17/
b.	______	☐1	☐2	18/	☐☐/☐☐/☐☐☐☐	19-26/
c.	______	☐1	☐2	27/	☐☐/☐☐/☐☐☐☐	28-35/
d.	______	☐1	☐2	36/	☐☐/☐☐/☐☐☐☐	37-44/
e.	______	☐1	☐2	45/	☐☐/☐☐/☐☐☐☐	46-53/
f.	______	☐1	☐2	54/	☐☐/☐☐/☐☐☐☐	55-62/
g.	______	☐1	☐2	63/	☐☐/☐☐/☐☐☐☐	64-71/
h.	______	☐1	☐2	72/	☐☐/☐☐/☐☐☐☐	73-80/

50. What is the rank of the highest-ranking military member in this family?

(Check One Category Box)

Enlisted Grades:

☐E-1 ☐E-2 ☐E-3 ☐E-4 ☐E-5 ☐E-6 ☐E-7 ☐E-8 ☐E-9 81-82/

Officer Grades:

☐O-1 ☐O-2 ☐O-3 ☐O-4 ☐O-5 ☐O-6 and above

Warrant Officer Grades:

☐W-1 ☐W-2 ☐W-3 ☐W-4

51. What was your <u>total</u> family income **IN 2003** BEFORE TAXES?

INCLUDE:

- **All earned income (BEFORE TAXES) including wages, salaries, tips, long-term disability benefits, combat pay and voluntary salary deferrals, retirement or other pension income before deductions for taxes or social security.**
- **Quarters subsistence and other allowances appropriate for the rank and status of military or civilian personnel whether received in cash or in kind. For dual military members include the BAH II of the senior member only. Include anything else of value, even if not taxable, that was received for providing services.**

DO NOT INCLUDE:

- **Cost of living allowance (COLA) received in high cost areas, alimony and child support, temporary duty allowances or reimbursements for educational expenses.**

(Check One)

☐1 Less than $ 25,000 *83/*

☐2 $ 25,000 – $ 49,999

☐3 $ 50,000 – $ 74,999

☐4 $ 75,000 – $ 99,999

☐5 $ 100,000 or more

52. What are the total annual earnings of the **civilian spouse** (if applicable) in 2003 BEFORE TAXES?

(Check One)

☐1 Less than $ 12,500 *84/*

☐2 $ 12,500 – $ 24,999

☐3 $ 25,000 – $ 36,999

☐4 $ 37,000 – $ 49,999

☐5 $ 50,000 or more

☐6 Not applicable. I don't have a civilian spouse.

☐7 Civilian spouse did not work outside the home.

53. What are your total current child care expenditures for the child whose name appears on the survey cover?

$ ☐ , ☐☐☐ ***(Round to the nearest dollar)*** *85-88/*

Per: ***(Check One)***

☐1 Week

☐2 Month *89/*

CARD 04

CARD 05 5-6/

1-4/

54. What are your total current expenditures for child care for <u>all</u> dependent children living with you including the child whose name appears on the survey cover? ***(Do not include private school tuition for school age children, but do include the cost of before- and after-school care.)***

$ ☐ , ☐☐☐ ***(Round to the nearest dollar)*** 7-10/

Per: ***(Check One)***

☐1 Week

☐2 Month 11/

55. For a child the age of the child whose name appears on the survey cover, how does the cost of off-base center care compare with DoD center care in the area in which you are now living?

(Check One) 12/

☐1 More expensive than DoD center care

☐2 The same as DoD center care

☐3 Less expensive than DoD center care

☐4 Don't know

56. For a child the age of the child whose name appears on the survey cover, how does the cost of off-base family child care compare with DoD home or family child care here?

(Check One) 13/

☐1 More expensive than DoD family child care

☐2 The same as DoD family child care

☐3 Less expensive than DoD family child care

☐4 Don't know

57. How do the costs of DoD home or family child care compare with DoD center care?

(Check One) 14/

☐1 DoD family child care is more expensive than DoD center care

☐2 DoD family child care is the same as DoD center care

☐3 DoD family child care is less expensive than DoD center care

☐4 Don't know

58. Will your provider care for the child whose name appears on the survey cover when he/she is sick?

(Check One) 15/

☐1 Yes → ***Skip to Question 59***

☐2 No

58a. If no, if your child was sick, would you be willing to pay an extra amount for care when the regular provider wouldn't accept the child (equivalent to the same amount you currently pay daily)?

(Check One) 16/

☐1 Yes

☐2 No

59. Who completed this questionnaire?

(Check One) 17/

☐1 Active duty military member (father)

☐2 Active duty military member (mother)

☐3 Civilian Spouse of active duty military member

☐4 Both parents

☐5 Someone else

Who? ______________________________ 18/

Continue on Next Page →

CARD 05

Section 5: Questions about Children Aged 6-12

60. Is the child whose name appears on the survey cover currently attending school in grades 1-8?

(Check One) 19/

- ☐1 No, child is too young. ***You are finished!***
- ☐2 No, child is being homeschooled. → ***Please answer Questions 61 - 72***
- ☐3 Yes, child is enrolled in grades 1-8. → ***Please answer Questions 61 - 72***

Summer Care for Children Aged 6-12

61. Please check all child care arrangements you used last summer for the child whose name appears on the survey cover.

(Check All That Apply)

- ☐1 DoD Summer camp program 20/
- ☐2 Civilian summer camp program 21/
- ☐3 Community recreation program, swimming pool, or supervised playground 22/
- ☐4 School activities program 23/
- ☐5 Civilian day care center 24/
- ☐6 DoD home or family child care (FCC) 25/
- ☐7 Civilian family child care 26/
- ☐8 Cared for by an older brother or sister 27/
- ☐9 Stayed with another relative (other than a brother or sister, e.g., grandparent) 28/
- ☐10 Stayed with a neighbor or a friend 29-30/
- ☐11 Parental care 31-32/
- ☐12 Took care of him / herself 33-34/
- ☐13 Other (Please Specify): ______________________ 35-36/ 37/

62. How satisfied are you with the arrangement you used last summer for the most hours per week for the child whose name appears on the survey cover?

(Check One) 38/

- ☐1 Very satisfied
- ☐2 Satisfied
- ☐3 Not completely satisfied
- ☐4 Dissatisfied
- ☐5 Very Dissatisfied

CARD 05

63. If less than very satisfied, what problems do you have with this arrangement? PLEASE PRINT CLEARLY.

____ 39/

____

64. Thinking about the arrangement you used <u>last summer</u> for the most hours weekly for the child whose name appears on the survey cover, would you have preferred another arrangement?

- ☐1 Yes 40/
- ☐2 No → ***Skip to Question 67, Next Page***

65. If yes, what other arrangement would you have preferred?

(Check One) 41-42/

- ☐1 DoD vacation camp program
- ☐2 Civilian vacation camp program
- ☐3 Community recreation program, swimming pool or supervised playground
- ☐4 School activities program
- ☐5 Civilian day care center
- ☐6 DoD home or family child care (FCC)
- ☐7 Civilian family child care
- ☐8 Cared for by an older brother or sister
- ☐9 Stayed with another relative (other than a brother or sister, e.g., grandparent)
- ☐10 Stayed with a neighbor or a friend
- ☐11 Parental care / took time off
- ☐12 Took care of him / herself
- ☐13 Other (Please Specify):

________________________ 43/

____

66. What stopped you from using this preferred arrangement?

(Check All That Apply)

- ☐1 Too expensive 44/
- ☐2 Hours not convenient 45/
- ☐3 Location not convenient 46/
- ☐4 Quality not high enough 47/
- ☐5 Lack of availability: no openings 48/
- ☐6 Provider couldn't accommodate my other children 49/
- ☐7 Preferred caretaker (self, relative, sibling) not available to provide care 50/
- ☐8 Other (Please Specify): ________________________ 51/ 52/
- ☐9 No reason 53/

CARD 05

Care during School Breaks and Holidays (During the School Year)

67. Please check all arrangements you used to care for the child whose name appears on the survey cover during the most recent school break or holiday (other than summer).

(Check All That Apply)

- ☐1 DoD vacation camp program 54/
- ☐2 Civilian vacation camp program 55/
- ☐3 Community recreation program or supervised playground 56/
- ☐4 School activities program 57/
- ☐5 Civilian day care center 58/
- ☐6 DoD home or family child care (FCC) 59/
- ☐7 Civilian family child care 60/
- ☐8 Cared for by an older brother or sister 61/
- ☐9 Stayed with another relative (other than a brother or sister, e.g., grandparent) 62/
- ☐10 Stayed with a neighbor or a friend 63-64/
- ☐11 Parental care / took time off 65-66/
- ☐12 Took care of him / herself 67-68/
- ☐13 Other (Please Specify): 69-70/

______________________________ 71/

____

68. How satisfied were you with the child care arrangement you used during the most recent school break or holiday (other than summer) for the most hours per week for the child whose name appears on the survey cover?

(Check One) 72/

- ☐1 Very satisfied
- ☐2 Satisfied
- ☐3 Not completely satisfied
- ☐4 Dissatisfied
- ☐5 Very Dissatisfied

69. If less than very satisfied, what problems do you have with this arrangement? PLEASE PRINT CLEARLY.

____ 73/

____

____

____

70. Thinking about the child care arrangement you used during the most recent school break or holiday (other than summer) for the most hours weekly for the child whose name appears on the survey cover, would you have preferred another arrangement?

(Check One) 74/

- ☐1 Yes
- ☐2 No → ***You are finished!***

CARD 05

71. If yes, what other child care arrangement would you have preferred?

(Check One) *75-76/*

- ☐1 DoD vacation camp program
- ☐2 Civilian vacation camp program
- ☐3 Community recreation program, swimming pool, or supervised playground
- ☐4 School activities program
- ☐5 Civilian day care center
- ☐6 DoD home or family child care (FCC)
- ☐7 Civilian family child care
- ☐8 Cared for by an older brother or sister
- ☐9 Stayed with another relative (other than a brother or sister, e.g., grandparent)
- ☐10 Stayed with a neighbor or a friend
- ☐11 Parental care / took time off
- ☐12 Took care of him / herself
- ☐13 Other (Please Specify): ____________________ *77/*

____

72. What stopped you from using this preferred arrangement?

(Check All That Apply)

- ☐1 Too expensive *78/*
- ☐2 Hours not convenient *79/*
- ☐3 Location not convenient *80/*
- ☐4 Quality not high enough *81/*
- ☐5 Lack of availability: no openings *82/*
- ☐6 Provider couldn't accommodate my other children *83/*
- ☐7 Preferred caretaker (self, relative, sibling) not available to provide care *84/*
- ☐8 Other (Please Specify): ____________________ *85/* *86/*
- ☐9 No reason *87/*

THANK YOU FOR COMPLETING THIS SURVEY!!

Please place your completed survey in the envelope provided and mail it to the RAND Corporation.

No Postage Needed!

88-89/

90/

CARD 05

References

Blau, D. M., *The Child Care Problem: An Economic Analysis*, New York, N.Y.: The Russell Sage Foundation, 2001.

Campbell, N. D., J. Appelbaum, K. Martinson, and E. Martin, *Be All That We Can Be: Lessons from the Military for Improving Our Nation's Child Care System*, Washington, D.C.: National Women's Law Center, 2000.

Defense Manpower Data Center (DMDC), *Status of Forces Survey of Active Duty Members*, CD-ROM, Arlington, Va.: Department of Defense, Defense Manpower Data Center, 2004.

Gates, S. M., G. L. Zellman, and J. S. Moini, with M. Suttorp, *Examining Child Care Need Among Military Families*, Santa Monica, Calif.: RAND Corporation, TR-279-OSD, 2006.

Harrell, M. C., N. Lim, L. W. Castaneda, and D. Golinelli, *Working Around the Military: Challenges to Military Spouse Employment and Education*, Santa Monica, Calif.: RAND Corporation, MG-196-OSD, 2004.

Hosek, J. R., B. J. Asch, C. C. Fair, C. W. Martin, and M. G. Mattock, *Married to the Military: The Employment and Earnings of Military Wives Compared with Those of Civilian Wives*, Santa Monica, Calif.: RAND Corporation, MR-1565-OSD, 2002.

Jehn, C., Assistant Secretary of Defense, Force Management and Personnel, "Determining the Five-Year Demand for Child Care Services Within the Department of Defense," letter to the Honorable Les Aspin, Chairman, Committee on Armed Forces, House of Representatives, December 31, 1990.

Kiger, P. K., "A Case for Child Care," *Workforce Management*, April 2004, pp. 34–40 (http://www.workforce.com/section/02/feature/23/68/05/; last accessed February 2006).

Macro International, Inc., *1999 Family Child Care Research Project Report and Recommendations,* Calverton, Md.: Macro International, Inc., 1999.

Military HOMEFRONT Web site (http://www.mfrc-dodqol.org/MCY/mm_cdc.htm; last accessed March 23, 2005).

Office of the Secretary of Defense, Force Management and Personnel, *Potential Demand for Child Care Within the Department of Defense and a Plan to Expand Availability: A Report to Congress,* U.S. Department of Defense, July 1992.

Queralt, M., and A. D. Witte, "Estimating the Unmet Need for Services: A Middling Approach, *Social Services Review,* December 1999, pp. 524–559.

U.S. Department of Defense, "Military Child Development Program Potential Need Memo," April 2002.

U.S. Department of Defense, Office of Family Policy, *Need for Child Care Spaces by Service,* March 2000.

U.S. Department of Defense, U.S. Inspector General, *Report of Inspection on Military Service Child Care Programs,* Washington, D.C.: U.S. Department of Defense, September 1990.

Zellman, G. L., and S. M. Gates, *Examining the Cost of Military Child Care,* Santa Monica, Calif.: RAND Corporation, MR-1415-OSD, 2002.

Zellman, G. L., A. S. Johansen, L. S. Meredith, and M. Selvin, *Improving the Delivery of Military Child Care: An Analysis of Current Operations and New Approaches,* Santa Monica, Calif.: RAND Corporation, R-4145-FMP, 1992.